# *Jonathan Edwards*

An Introduction to America's Greatest
Theologian/Philosopher

by

W. Gary Crampton, Th.D.
author of *What the Puritans Taught*

Edited by Dr. Don Kistler

Soli Deo Gloria Publications
*. . . for instruction in righteousness . . .*

Soli Deo Gloria Publications
A division of Soli Deo Gloria Ministries, Inc.
P.O. Box 451, Morgan PA 15064
(412) 221-1901/FAX 221-1902
www.SDGbooks.com

\*

\*

ISBN 1-57358-160-7

\*

The author uses both the King James Version and
the New King James Version of the Bible in his book.

\*

Library of Congress Cataloging-in-Publication Data

Crampton, W. Gary, 1943-
  Meet Jonathan Edwards : an introduction to America's greatest
theologian/philosopher / by W. Gary Crampton ; edited by Don
Kistler.
      p. cm.
  Includes bibliographical references.
  ISBN 1-57358-160-7 (alk. paper)
  1. Edwards, Jonathan, 1703-1758. I. Kistler, Don. II. Title.
BX7260.E3C66 2004
230'.58'092--dc22
                                        2004006028

# Contents

This book is dedicated to the late Edwardsean scholar, Dr. John H. Gerstner. It was he who first challenged me to read Edwards; and for this I will be eternally grateful.

# Introduction

In Matthew 23:8–10, it is the Lord Jesus Christ Himself who warns us, "But you, do not be called 'Rabbi'; for one is your Teacher, the Christ, and you are all brethren. Do not call anyone on earth your father; for One is your Father, He who is in heaven. And do not be called teachers; for one is your Teacher, the Christ." In other words, no man is to be elevated to the level of Christ. He is *sui generis* ("one of a kind"). He is unique; He is the only Teacher of men. Yet, as the author of Hebrews tells us, there are certain men whose godly example we are to emulate: "Remember those who rule over you, who have spoken the Word of God to you, whose faith follow, considering the outcome of their conduct" (13:7). In fact, in Hebrews 11, we have, given under the inspiration of the Holy Spirit, a list of faithful men who are examples for us to follow.

Jonathan Edwards was such a man. He was a theo-centric-minded man; he thought biblically. In the words of the Apostle Paul, his mind was "set on things above" (Colossians 3:2). Edwards was a man of great spiritual insight, and one of the greatest thinkers in the history of the Christian church. As Charles Andrews stated, "The story of Jonathan Edwards is less the history of a life than the analysis of a mind." And as Henry Rogers wrote, Edwards was likely "the most perfect specimen of the intellectual athlete the world has ever seen."[1]

Following on the heels of the Protestant Reformation (especially John Calvin) and the seventeenth-century Puritans, Jonathan Edwards continued in the Puritan

---

[1] Cited in John H. Gerstner, *The Rational Biblical Theology of Jonathan Edwards*, Introduction. [For all publishing information on any footnote, see the bibliography at the conclusion of this work.]

tradition, expressed so admirably in the Westminster Shorter Catechism (Q. 1), that "man's chief end is to glorify God, and to enjoy Him forever." David Brand wrote: "It is evident that all of Edwards's life and thought moved inexorably toward one grand final focus, the glory of God."[2] Jonathan Edwards was a "God-intoxicated" man who was "mastered" by the Word of God.[3] Theology, wrote Iain Murray, "belonged to the warp and woof of his life." He was "a man who put faithfulness to the Word of God before every other consideration."[4] As one student of the Puritans put it, Edwards always operated within a "Biblical cage."[5] The entirety of his life was involved in "a quest for godliness." "All his life," wrote J. I. Packer, "he labored, fearlessly and tirelessly, to understand and apply the Bible. . . . All his life he fed his soul on the Bible; and all his life he fed his flock on the Bible."[6] And as another Edwardsean scholar aptly stated, "The simplest way to define Puritanism is to say it is what Edwards was."[7]

It is beyond serious question, as Samuel Davies suggested, that Jonathan Edwards is "the profoundest reasoner, and the greatest divine . . . that America ever produced."[8] He was "America's premier philosopher-theologian."[9] He was "America's Theologian"[10]; "the

---

[2] David C. Brand, *The Profile of the Last Puritan*, p. 146.

[3] Carl W. Bogue, *Jonathan Edwards and the Covenant of Grace*, pp. 42, 50.

[4] Iain. H. Murray, *Jonathan Edwards: A New Biography*, pp. xx, 471.

[5] Peter Gay, as cited in Gerstner, *The Rational Biblical Theology of Jonathan Edwards*, I:102.

[6] J. I. Packer, *A Quest for Godliness*, p. 310.

[7] Cited in Chard Powers Smith, *Yankees and God*, p. 247. The statement is that of Perry Miller.

[8] Cited in Murray, *Jonathan Edwards: A New Biography*, p. xv.

[9] Stephen Stein, Edwards, *Works* (Yale), 5:1.

[10] Robert W. Jenson, *American's Theologian*, p. 1.

American Augustine"[11]; "the American Calvin."[12]
"Jonathan Edwards stands out," said B. B. Warfield, "as
the one figure of real greatness in the intellectual life of
colonial America." He was "the greatest of American
Calvinists," a man who had a "remarkable sense and taste
for divine things." He was a man whose "analytical sub-
tlety has probably never been surpassed."[13] Simply
stated, Jonathan Edwards was the Puritan Sage, "a mind
in love with God."[14]

Edwards expressed this in his own words as follows:

> God is the highest good of the reasonable creatures; and
> the enjoyment of Him is the only happiness with
> which our souls can be satisfied. To go to heaven, fully
> to enjoy God, is infinitely better than the most pleasant
> accommodations here. Fathers and mothers, husbands,

---

[11] Gerald R. McDermott, *One Holy Happy Society*, p. 177.

[12] Philip Schaff, *History of the Christian Church*, VIII:544.

[13] Benjamin B. Warfield, *Studies in Theology*, pp. 515–516, 528.
Warfield cites F. J. E. Woodbridge here with approbation.

[14] John Piper, *God's Passion for His Glory*, p. 77; see also John
Piper, *The Supremacy of God in Preaching*, p. 66. It is simply because
Jonathan Edwards was "a mind in love with God" that numbers of
those outside of the Christian faith have such a different opinion of
him. George Lyon, for example, bemoans the fact that Edwards,
who could have been "the greatest metaphysician America has yet
produced," chose to study theology instead, a discipline which Lyon
sees as a "sublime and barbarous theology." Then too, Clarence
Darrow, known for his involvement in the infamous Scopes Trial, is
another antagonist of Jonathan Edwards. "Nothing but a distorted or
diseased mind," wrote Darrow, "could have produced his 'Sinners in
the Hands of an Angry God.' " This is also the opinion of the
universalist theologian, George MacDonald, who wrote: "From all
copies of Jonathan Edwards' portrait of [the absolute sovereignty of]
God, however faded by time, however softened by the use of less
glaring pigments, I turn with loathing." These citations are found
in Nancy Manspeaker, *Jonathan Edwards: A Bibliographical Synopsis*,
pp. 48, 118–119; Brand, *Profile of the Last Puritan*, pp. 23, 29; and
John Piper, *The Pleasures of God, pp.* 170–171.

wives, or children, or the company of earthly friends,
are but shadows; but the enjoyment of God is the substance. These are but scattered beams; but God is the
sun. These are but streams; but God is the fountain.
These are but drops; but God is the ocean.[15]

These things being so, we who live in the early years
of the twenty-first century would do well to study the
teachings of this Puritan Sage. The reason being, as suggested by S. I. Prime, that "the message he preached is
relevant to every age: It has the life of Christ in it; it
subordinates the reason to divine authority, and adores
the Holy Spirit. . . . His [Edwards'] theology had
revivals and repentance, and salvation from hell, in it;
and this made it, and makes it, and will keep it divine
theology till Christ is all in all."[16]

---

[15] Jonathan Edwards, *Works*, II:244
[16] Cited in Murray, *Jonathan Edwards: A New Biography*, pp. xxx-xxxi.

# 1

## *Jonathan Edwards, the Man*

Jonathan Edwards was born on October 5, 1703, in East Windsor, Connecticut. He was the fifth child, and the only son among eleven children, of Timothy and Esther Edwards. Jonathan's father was the Congregational pastor in East Windsor. He had begun his pastoral ministry in 1694, a position which he held until 1755. Jonathan's mother was the daughter of the renowned pastor of Northampton, Massachusetts, Solomon Stoddard, the "pope of the Connecticut Valley,"[1] a man who would later play an important part in Jonathan Edwards's life.

Timothy Edwards taught his very precocious son, along with a number of other boys in his congregation, the Bible, Hebrew, Greek, Latin, and other disciplines from an early age. The particular emphasis of pastor Edwards was that of the Christian faith, and the need of these young students to "close with Christ," that is, to put their full faith and trust in Him as Lord and Savior. Young Jonathan was privileged to see two seasons of revival under his father's ministry at East Windsor. Speaking of his own personal experience, he wrote:

---

[1] This unofficial title was given to Solomon Stoddard due to the "genuine reality of his overwhelming influence, both on his people and those of the neighboring parishes" (Samuel Logan, "The Doctrine of Justification in the Theology of Jonathan Edwards," *Westminster Theological Journal* 46 [1984], p. 29).

> I had a variety of concerns and exercises about my
> soul from my childhood; but I had two more re-
> markable seasons of awakening before I met with
> that change by which I was brought to those new
> dispositions, and the new sense of things that I have
> since had. The first time was when I was a  boy,
> some years before I went to college, at a time of
> remarkable awakening in my father's congregation. I
> was then very much affected for many months, and
> concerned about the things of religion, and my
> soul's salvation; and was abundant in religious duties.
> I used to pray five times a day in secret, and to
> spend much time in religious conversation with
> other boys; and used to meet with them to pray to-
> gether. I experienced I know not what kind of de-
> light in religion. My mind was much engaged in it,
> and had much self-righteous pleasure, and it was my
> delight to abound in religious duties. I, with some of
> my schoolmates, joined together and built a booth
> in a swamp, in a very retired spot, for a place of
> prayer. And besides, I had particular secret places of
> my own in the woods where I used to retire by my-
> self, and was from time to time much affected. . . .
> I am ready to think many are deceived with such af-
> fections, and such kind of delight as I then had in
> religion, and mistake it for [saving] grace.[2]

Notably, Jonathan Edwards here contrasts a form of
temporary "seasons of awakening" in which he experi-
enced a kind of "self-righteous pleasure" and "religious
duties," which were devoid of saving grace, with his
later conversion. At this early age, he was a very "religious" person, but not yet justified by grace alone
through faith alone in Christ alone.

In 1716, at the age of thirteen, Edwards entered the
Collegiate School at Connecticut (later to be called
"Yale" after Elihu Yale), where he studied a number of
subjects, including theology and philosophy. Here he

---

[2] Edwards, *Works*, I:xii.

also studied the Westminster Confession of Faith, along with the Larger and Shorter Catechisms, agreeing with and embracing as his own the Reformed and Calvinistic theology taught therein.[3] Conrad Cherry wrote that "Edwards was a Calvinist theologian; and, as a Calvinist theologian, he claimed the heritage of his New England forefathers. . . . All five of [the Synod of] Dort's points were claimed by Edwards as necessary defenses of God's power and glory in the salvation of man."[4]

Even while still young, Jonathan Edwards began "to study with his pen in his hand." He studied prayerfully, developing thoughts which he wanted to preserve in writing. As witnessed by his literary productivity (which included some extremely astute papers, even

---

[3] Edwards, *Works*, I:cxxi; Murray, *Jonathan Edwards: A New Biography*, 468; and Holmes Rolston, III, *John Calvin Versus the Westminster Confession*, 15-20. Warfield pointed out that Jonathan Edwards, as an independent thinker, did not adopt the doctrines of Calvinism because they were taught by John Calvin. Rather, he believed the doctrines of Calvinism because he was convinced that they are the doctrines taught in the Word of God. Edwards "should be understood to be not a blind follower of Calvin, but a convinced defender of Calvinism." See Warfield, *Studies in Theology*, 531. Edwards's own words on this matter are, "I should not take it at all amiss to be called a Calvinist, for distinction's sake; though I utterly disclaim a dependence on Calvin, or believing the doctrines which I hold because he believed and taught them; and cannot justly be charged with believing everything just as he taught" (*Works* [Yale], 1:131).

[4] Conrad Cherry, *Jonathan Edwards: A Reappraisal*, 3, 189. See also Edwards, *Works*, I:86–89. The reference to the five points of the Synod of Dort has to do with the five points of Calvinism, as set forth in the acrostic TULIP: T—total depravity; U—unconditional election; L—limited atonement; I—irresistible grace; P—perseverance of the saints. For more on this subject, see David N. Steele and Curtis C. Thomas, *The Five Points of Calvinism*.

from his youth[5] ), he continued this kind of study for the rest of his life. Later, as a minister of the gospel, he wrote:

> My method of study . . . has been very much by writing; applying myself, in this way, to improve every important hint; pursuing the clue to my utmost, when anything in reading, meditation, or conversation, has been suggested to my mind, that seemed to promise light in any weighty point; thus penning what appeared to me my best thoughts, on innumerable subjects, for my own benefit.[6]

But all of Edwards's "best thoughts, on innumerable subjects, for my own benefit," even from his early years, were governed by his zeal to reconcile "all of life and learning to the dictates of God's law as contained in Scripture." Even with his inquiring mind that knew no boundaries, scientific or literary, the main goal of Jonathan Edwards was to be an "instrument in the cause of his Christ."[7]

Edwards graduated from college in 1720 as the top student in the class and gave the valedictory address in Latin. He continued his studies for several more years preparing for the ministry. He was licensed to preach at

---

[5] For example, (probably) in his late teens he wrote such articles as "Of Insects," "Of the Rainbow," "Of Light Rays," and "Of Atoms," and perhaps the "Spider Letter." There is some question among Edwardsian scholars as to when some of these essays were written, but no matter what the age of the writer—early teens, late teens, or even early twenties—they are the work of a precocious young man.

[6] Edwards, *Works*, I:clxxiv. Interestingly, John Calvin also studied with his pen in his hand. In his *Institutes of the Christian Religion* ("John Calvin to the Reader"), Calvin wrote: "I count myself one of the number of those who write as they learn and learn as they write."

[7] Eds., in Edwards, *A Jonathan Edwards Reader*, pp. vii–x.

the age of nineteen and completed his Master of Arts in divinity in 1723. He accepted a call to a Presbyterian church in New York and ministered there for eight months. While in New York, he wrote of his spiritual growth:

> My longings after God and holiness were much increased. Pure and humble, holy and heavenly, Christianity appeared exceeding amiable to me. I felt a burning desire to be in everything a complete Christian, and conformed to the blessed image of Christ; and that I might live, in all things, according to the pure, sweet and blessed rules of the gospel.
>
> I had then, and at other times, the greatest delight in the holy Scriptures of any book whatsoever. Oftentimes in reading it every word seemed to touch my heart. I felt a harmony between something in my heart and those sweet and powerful words. I seemed often to see so much light exhibited by every sentence, and such a refreshing food communicated, that I could not get along in reading; often dwelling long on one sentence, to see the wonders contained in it; and yet almost every sentence seemed to be full of wonders.[8]

Jonathan Edwards returned to Yale as a tutor for a period of two years. Then, in 1726, he resigned his teaching position to accept a call as the assistant pastor to his grandfather, Solomon Stoddard, who had pastored the Congregational Church of Northampton since 1672. Interestingly, the Congregationalist Stoddard and the Congregationalist New England churches accommodated to a form of Presbyterianism in the Saybrook Confession of 1708, wherein the teaching elders of the churches agreed to meet two times a year to discuss the duties of their office and the common interest of the churches.

---

[8] Edwards, *Works*, I:xiii–xiv.

Further, Jonathan Edwards, who endorsed the teachings of the Westminster Standards, also believed the Presbyterian form of church government to be the "most agreeable to the Word of God."[9]

It was probably in the spring of 1721 that Jonathan Edwards was genuinely converted.[10] According to his own personal account, the doctrine of God's absolute sovereignty, especially in matters of election and reprobation, had previously seemed to him as a "horrible doctrine." Then, however, by the grace of God, said Edwards, "I seemed to be convinced, and fully satisfied, as to the sovereignty of God and His justice in thus eternally disposing of men according to His sovereign pleasure. . . . However, my mind rested in it; and it put an end to all those cavils and objections. And there has been a wonderful alteration in my mind, with respect to the doctrine of God's sovereignty, from that day to this; so that I scarce ever have found so much as the rising of an objection against it." Rather, he went on to say, "I have often, since that first conviction, had quite another kind of sense of God's sovereignty than I had then. I have often since had not only a conviction, but a delightful conviction. The doctrine has very often appeared exceedingly pleasant, bright, and sweet. Absolute sovereignty is what I love to ascribe to God."[11]

It was a comprehension of 1 Timothy 1:17 that led Jonathan Edwards to this conviction and new sense of divine things. He wrote:

---

[9] Edwards, *Works*, I:cxxi. In a letter to the church committee in Northampton, Edwards spoke of "Mr. Stoddard's Presbyterian principles," with which he agreed (*Works* (Yale), 16:314).

[10] Murray, *Jonathan Edwards: A New Biography*, pp. 33–35.

[11] Edwards, *Works*, I:xii–xiii.

> The first instance that I remember of that sort of inward, sweet delight in God and divine things, that I have lived much in since, was on reading those words, 1 Timothy 1:17: "Now unto the King eternal, immortal, invisible, the only wise God, be honor and glory forever and ever. Amen." As I read the words, there came into my soul, and was as it were diffused through it, a sense of the glory of the Divine Being; a new sense, quite different from anything I ever experienced before. Never any words of Scripture seemed to me as these words did. I thought with myself, how excellent a Being that was, and how happy I should be if I might enjoy that God, and be rapt up to Him in heaven; and be as it were swallowed up in Him forever! I kept saying, and as it were singing, over these words of Scripture to myself; and went to pray to God that I might enjoy Him; and prayed in a manner quite different from what I used to do, with a new sort of affection.[12]

As David Brand points out in his *Profile of the Last Puritan* (p.13), Edwards's experience was not some "subjective, mystical experience, but an objective experience rooted in the Bible." The evidence of a genuine conversion was witnessed to by the intensity of Edwards's inner life:

> After this [conversion] my sense of divine things gradually increased, and became more lively, and more of the inward sweetness. The appearance of everything was altered; there seemed to be, as it were, a calm, sweet cast or appearance of divine glory in almost everything. God's excellency, His wisdom, His purity and love, seemed to appear in everything. . . . I was almost always constantly in ejaculatory prayer, wherever I was. Prayer seemed to be natural to me, as the breath by which the inward

---

[12] Edwards, *Works*, I:xiii.

> burnings of my heart had vent. The delights which I now felt in those things of religion were of an exceeding different kind from those before mentioned, that I had when a boy; and what I then had no more notion of than one born blind has of pleasant and beautiful colors. They were of a more inward, pure, soul-animating and refreshing nature. Those former delights never reached the heart; and did not rise from any sight of the divine excellency of the things of God; or any taste of the soul-satisfying and life-giving good there is in them.[13]

It was also during these early years when Jonathan Edwards wrote his "Resolutions," which he viewed as "firm determinations," or "instructions for life, [and] maxims to be followed in all respects. . . . The ultimate intention of [which] was to produce a soul fit for eternity with God."[14] In the words of John Piper, these resolutions "capture some of the remarkable passion of this season of his life." There was a sort of "single-mindedness that governed his life and enabled him to accomplish amazing things."[15] Here are a few examples: Resolution #1: "Resolved, that I will do whatsoever I think to be most to the glory of God, and my own good, profit, and pleasure, in the whole of my duration; without any consideration of the time, whether now, or ever so many myriads of ages hence. Resolved to do whatever I think to be my duty, and most for the good and advantage of mankind in general. Resolved, so to do, whatever difficulties I meet with, how many so ever, and how great so ever." Resolution #4: "Resolved, never to do any manner of thing, whether in soul or body, less or more, than what tends to the glory of God." Resolution #7:

[13] Edwards, *Works*, I:xiii.
[14] George Claghorn, in Jonathan Edwards, *Works* (Yale), 16:741, 743.
[15] Piper, *God's Passion for His Glory*, p. 52.

"Resolved, never to do anything which I should be afraid to do if it were the last hour of my life." Resolution #28: "Resolved, to study the Scriptures so steadily, constantly, and frequently, as that I may find and plainly perceive myself to grow in the knowledge of the same."[16] And the thing about these resolutions, as the late John Gerstner pointed out, is that they "were conscientiously carried out in practice the rest of his life."[17]

It was also at this time that Jonathan Edward began to write his "Miscellanies." These were notes, articles, and papers that he wrote on various subjects (theological, philosophical, scientific), which, in a sense, trace his intellectual development and maturation. Some of these were very short, and others were very lengthy. He added to these throughout his life.[18]

Noteworthy is the fact, as evidenced by his numerous writings, that Jonathan Edwards was a strong advocate of the Reformed principle of *sola Scriptura*. He taught that all studies, regardless of the subject matter, were to be judged by Scripture alone. Nothing stands in judgment over the Word of God. It has a monopoly on truth. Scrip-

---

[16] Edwards, *Works* (Yale), 16:753–759. There were seventy resolutions in all. Although it was not written down as a resolution, Edwards also resolved to use his time with the utmost care. As Claghorn stated, "Time management was a major concern to Edwards. His aim was to rise early, work late, and fill every moment with constructive activity." Edwards even viewed sleeping as a potential waste of time, to be cut to a minimum, so that he could more fully accomplish what he believed God had given him to accomplish (*Works* [Yale], 16:744).

[17] John H. Gerstner, *The Rational Biblical Theology of Jonathan Edwards*, I:13. Edwards, being the humble man that he was, was not as confident about his practice of these resolutions. In his diary he wrote: "I take up a strong resolution, but how soon does it weaken!" (Edwards, *A Jonathan Edwards Reader*, p. 267).

[18] Edwards' first "Miscellany" was written in 1722, and his last in 1758, the year of his death.

ture is all-sufficient not only to lead one to a sound and
saving knowledge of God through Jesus Christ, but also to
justify all knowledge and to interpret every area of life.[19]
This was the biblical cage in which he operated. Wrote
John Smith: "Edwards accepted totally the tradition
established by the Reformers with respect to the absolute primacy and authority of the Bible, and he could
approach the biblical writings with that conviction of
their inerrancy and literal truth."[20] As stated by David
Brand:

> The Edwardsian legacy represents a call to re-estab-
> lish theology as the queen of the sciences, not in
> terms of a rigidity that stifles scholarship or scien-
> tific inquiry, but rather in the form of a lucid and
> forceful assertion of the Holy Scriptures as the
> fountainhead of all human academic endeavor.[21]

This is also attested to in Edwards's diary (started at
the age of nineteen), which he (like many Puritans) kept
as a record or journal of his spiritual state.

Then too, it was also during these years that Jonathan
Edwards met Sarah Pierrepont. He recognized in this
young girl a love of and desire to please God that was

---

[19] Jonathan Edwards, sermon on 2 Timothy 3:16 and Miscellany
350. Henceforth, whenever a sermon or a miscellany of Jonathan
Edwards is cited in this book, it is referenced from one of the works
found in the bibliography, without (necessarily) noting the biblio-
graphic work in which it is found. This sermon, for example, is
found in Alexander Grosart, *Selections from the Unpublished Writings of
Jonathan Edwards*, pp. 191–196; and the Miscellany is found in
Gerstner, *The Rational Biblical Theology of Jonathan Edwards*, I:109.
[20] John E. Smith, *Review of Metaphysics* (December 1976), as cited
in Sproul, Gerstner, and Lindsley, *Classical Apologetics*, p. 243.
[21] Brand, *Profile of the Last Puritan*, p. 146. See also Victor Budgen,
*The Charismatics and the Word of God*, pp. 165–178.

similar to his own. When he was twenty, and she but
thirteen, Jonathan wrote of Sarah:

> They say there is a young lady in New Haven who is
> beloved of that Great Being who made and rules the
> world, and there are certain seasons in which this
> Great Being, in some way or other invisible, comes
> to her and fills her mind with exceeding sweet
> delight, and that she hardly cares for any thing,
> except to meditate on Him—that she expects after
> a while to be received up where He is, to be raised
> up out of the world and caught up into heaven;
> being assured that He loves her too well to let her
> remain at a distance from Him always. There she is
> to dwell with Him, and to be ravished with His love
> and delight forever. Therefore, if you present all
> the world before her, with the richest of its
> treasures, she disregards it and cares not for it, and
> is unmindful of any pain or affliction. She has a
> strange sweetness in her mind, and singular purity
> in her affections; is most just and conscientious in
> all her conduct; and you could not persuade her to do
> anything wrong or sinful if you would give her all
> the world, lest she should offend this Great Being.
> She is of a wonderful sweetness, calmness and uni-
> versal benevolence of mind; especially after this
> great God has manifested Himself to her mind. She
> will sometimes go about from place to place,
> singing sweetly; and she seems to be always full of
> joy and pleasure; and no one knows for what. She
> loves to be alone, walking in the fields and groves,
> and seems to have someone invisible always con-
> versing with her.[22]

Four years later, in 1727, after Jonathan Edwards had
been installed as the assistant pastor at Northampton,
Sarah Pierrepont became Mrs. Jonathan Edwards.
Jonathan was twenty-three years old at the time and

---

[22] Cited in Murray, *Jonathan Edwards: A New Biography*, p. 92.

Sarah was seventeen. And in the next twenty-three years the Edwards would have eleven children of their own, three sons and eight daughters.[23]

John Gerstner sees somewhat of a parallel between the years of Edwards's ministry and those of the Lord Jesus Christ. There was a period of obscurity (1726–1733), followed by a period of popularity (1734–1744), followed by a period of opposition (1744–1758). The years of obscurity were those when Edwards was assisting his eminent grandfather, Solomon Stoddard. Years before Edwards accepted the call to the church in Northampton, Stoddard had introduced a view of the Lord's Supper wherein the sacrament might be a "converting ordinance." Church members with moral lives, yet who might not be genuinely converted, were encouraged to partake of the elements of the Lord's Supper which might, argued Stoddard, lead to their conversion. What resulted from this, however, was a general laxity in matters of the Christian faith, and somewhat of a faction between two groups within the congregation. (Stoddard is wrongly accused as being in favor of unregenerate non–church members taking the elements of this sacrament, but that is not the case. And even the Westminster Confession encourages those who are in doubt about their salvation to come to the table.)

Jonathan Edwards began his ministry at Northampton under these circumstances. Years later, his opposition to the "converting ordinance" view of the Lord's Supper would lead to his dismissal. Edwards took his calling

---

[23] Recognizing that, according to Scripture there is nothing sinful, *per se*, about having a slave (if treated in accordance with the Word of God), Jonathan Edwards possessed domestic slaves who served his family. He was, however, opposed to the slave trade (Edwards, *A Jonathan Edwards Reader*, pp. xxxiv, 296–297; *Works* (Yale), 16:10, 71–76).

very seriously. He entered into the work with a servant's heart, and a diligence to serve his Master. Along with his other pastoral duties, including the preaching and teaching of the Word of God, counseling, and writing various discourses, Edwards devoted himself to the study of Scripture. It was not uncommon for him to spend thirteen hours a day in his study. Some of this time was used in counseling various members of his congregation.[24] But most of it was taken up in study and prayer. According to Ava Chamberlain, "his lifelong pursuit [was] to draw near to God through an understanding of doctrine."[25]

And as noted, it was Edwards' practice to study prayerfully, with his pen in his hand. He did so, taking copious notes, and continually working on and adding to his "Notes on Scripture," "Types of the Messiah," and "Miscellanies." He also had a Bible with some 900 blank interleaved pages (his "Blank Bible"), in which he would write his comments on passages of Scripture. In all of his writings, he displayed "a mastery of the Biblical text achieved through regular study of the Bible."[26]

Jonathan Edwards was of the opinion that he could better promote the great ends of his ministry in this fashion. Edwards understood very well, as Robert Reymond writes, that "without that inner life which is produced only by much time spent in consideration of and mediation upon the Word of God in purposeful self-examination, and before the presence of the Lord in

---

[24] Stephen J. Nichols, *Jonathan Edwards: A Guided Tour of His Life and Thought*, p. 20. As Nichols points out, even though Jonathan Edwards was more at home with his books than with other people, he always took the time to visit and to meet with his parishioners, especially those who were "soul anxious." He was a good pastor.

[25] Ava Chamberlain, in Edwards, *Works* (Yale), 18:8.

[26] Stephen J. Stein, Introduction, Jonathan Edwards, *Works* (Yale), 15:25.

earnest prayer, [a minister of the Word of God] will
never obtain that blessed ministry which the Puritan
writers described as 'powerful,' 'painful' (that is, labori-
ous), and 'useful.' "[27] Edwards wrote:

> A true Christian doubtless delights in religious fel-
> lowship and Christian conversation, and finds much
> to affect his heart in it, but he also delights at times
> to retire from all mankind to converse with God . . .
> True religion disposes persons to be much alone in
> solitary places for holy mediation and prayer. So it
> wrought in Isaac (Genesis 24:63). And, which is
> much more, so it wrought in Jesus Christ. How of-
> ten do we read of His retiring into mountains and
> solitary places for holy converse with the Father. . .
> The most eminent divine favors which the saints
> obtained that we read of in Scripture were in their
> retirement. . . . [I]t is the nature of true grace . . .
> to delight in retirement, and secret converse with
> God.[28]

From early on in his own ministry Edwards said:

> I spent most of my time in thinking of divine
> things, year after year; often walking alone in the
> woods, and solitary places, for meditation, soliloquy,
> and prayer, and converse with God; and it was always
> my manner, at such times, to sing forth my con-
> templations. I was almost constantly in ejaculatory
> prayer, wherever I was. Prayer seemed to be natural
> to me, as the breath by which the inward burnings
> of my heart had vent.[29]

Prayer for Edwards was nothing more than "personal
communion with the Almighty." It was "a hallmark of his

[27] Robert L. Reymond, *Paul: Missionary Theologian*, p. 578.
[28] Edwards, *Works*, I:311–312.
[29] Jonathan Edwards, *Jonathan Edwards: Representative Selections*,
p. 61.

theology," and "an experience which Edwards sought on a daily basis."[30]

Jonathan Edwards was also a good family man. He spent time daily with his wife and children, allowing himself a season of relaxation in the midst of his family. Also, it was his daily practice to pray with them and to teach them the Word of God, always pressing upon them their need for Christ as Savior and Lord. Young children within a Christian family, taught Edwards, are the very best field for evangelism. In his sermon on Job 20:11, for example, he preached: "Persons when in their youth are ordinarily more easily awakened than afterward. Their minds are tender and it is a more easy thing to make impression upon them." This teaching was to bring forth fruit in the Edwards family, as ten of his eleven children later gave convincing evidence of saving faith.[31]

The continual fatherly concern of Jonathan Edwards for the spiritual state of his family is also evident in a letter he wrote to his sickly, married daughter Esther Edwards Burr, as late as 1753:

> I would not have you think that any strange thing has happened to you in this affliction: it is according to the course of things in this world that after the world's smiles some great affliction soon comes. God has now given you early and seasonable warning not at all to depend on worldly prosperity. Therefore I would advise, if it pleases God to restore you, to let upon no happiness here. Labor while you live to serve God and do what good you can, and endeavor to improve every dispensation to God's glory and your own spiritual good, and be content to do and bear all that God calls you to in this

---

[30] Claghorn, in Edwards, *Works* (Yale), 16:745.

[31] For more on the Edwards family and children, see Edna Gerstner, *Jonathan and Sarah: An Uncommon Union*, and Elisabeth Dodds, *Marriage to a Difficult Man*.

wilderness, and never expect to find this world anything better than a wilderness. Lay your account to
travel through it in weariness, painfulness, and
trouble, and wait for your rest and your prosperity
till hereafter, where they that die in the Lord rest
from their labors and enter into the joy of the Lord.
You are like to spend the rest of your life (if you
should get over this illness) at a great distance from
your parents; but care not much for that. If you
lived near us, yet our breath and yours would soon go
forth, and we should return to our dust, whither we
are all hastening. It is of infinitely more importance
to have the presence of an heavenly Father, and to
make progress towards an heavenly home. Let us
take care that we may meet there at last.[32]

Overall, the Edwards family was an example to the
church and society as a whole. Wrote James Hefley:

One of the most interesting studies ever made of
family influence traced the careers of the descendants of Jonathan Edwards, a famous Colonial minister, and Max Jukes, an outspoken unbeliever who
lived near Edwards. From Edwards and his devout
Christian wife came 729 descendants. They included 300 ministers, 65 college professors, 13 university presidents, 60 authors of good books, 3 U.S.
congressmen, and one vice-president of the United
States. The only known black sheep was Aaron
Burr, an Edwards grandson who departed from his
childhood faith and tried to overthrow the U.S.
government.[33] In contrast, Jukes married an unbeliever and they produced 1,026 known descendants.
Three hundred died early in life. A hundred went to
prison for an average of 13 years each. Around 200
were public prostitutes and another 100 were drunk-
ards. As a whole, the Jukes family was an enormous

---

[32] Edwards, *A Jonathan Edwards Reader*, p. 312.
[33] Aaron Burr (1756–1836) was tried for treason in 1807, and was ac-
quitted of the charge.

detriment to society and the Edwards clan was an
immeasurable asset.[34]

Solomon Stoddard died in 1729, and Jonathan
Edwards was called to be the pastor of the Northampton
church. He would serve in this capacity until 1750. "To
the pastoral care of this important congregation," wrote
B.B. Warfield, "Edwards gave himself with single-
hearted devotion."[35] His ministry flourished. He pastored his people, he preached the Word of God, and he
even mentored young candidates for the ministry. He
was also asked to preach in other Christian church gath-
erings. Based on the requests of his own Northampton
church members, some of his sermons were published
during this time. But it was during the first great awakening (1734–1735) that Edwards's years of popularity began.
The tremors of revival were felt over the next 15 years,
with the second great awakening occurring in the early
1740s. During this time, many persons, having heard the
deeply penetrating studies of Scripture ministered by
Edwards (and others), became very aware of their
"sottish" spiritual state.[36] "Scripture warnings [are] best
adapted to the conversion of sinners," taught Edwards in
a sermon on Luke 16:31. Particularly, "the consideration
of hell commonly is the first thing that rouses sleeping
sinners. By this means their sins are set before them," he
said in a sermon on Hebrews 9:12.

Edwards' sermon on Romans 3:19 ("The Justice of
God in the Damnation of Sinners") was preached during

---

[34] James C. Hefley, *Studies in Genesis*, p. 37.

[35] Warfield, *Studies in Theology*, p. 522.

[36] The Puritans referred to a person as being "sottish" who was dull
and listless concerning matters of the Christian faith. In his sermon
on Jeremiah 5:21–22, Edwards preached that "it is a sottish and
unreasonable thing for men not to fear God and tremble at His
presence."

the first great awakening. Edwards himself considered this to be his most powerful and effectual message. Commenting on the sermon, Sereno Dwight wrote:

> The sermon . . . literally stops the mouth of every reader and compels him, as he stands before his Judge, to admit, if he does not feel, the justice of his sentence. I know not where to find in any language a discourse so well adapted to strip the impenitent sinner of every excuse, to convince him of his guilt, and to bring him low before the justice and holiness of God. According to the estimate of Mr. Edwards, it was by far the most powerful and effectual of his discourses, and we scarcely know of any other sermon which has been favored with equal success.[37]

"Sinners in the Hands of an Angry God" (Edwards' most famous sermon) was preached in Enfield, Connecticut, on July 8, 1741. Numerous genuine conversions took place during these years through his preaching ministry.[38] Along this line of thought, Sereno Dwight, who wrote the *Memoirs of Jonathan Edwards*, once asked a man who had heard Edwards preach whether or not Edwards was an eloquent speaker. The man responded:

> He had no studied varieties of the voice, and no strong emphasis. He scarcely gestured, or even moved, and he made no attempt by the elegance of his style or the beauty of his pictures to gratify the taste and fascinate the imagination. But, if you

---

[37] Cited in John H. Gerstner, *Jonathan Edwards, Evangelist*, p. 25.
[38] Gerstner, *The Rational Biblical Theology of Jonathan Edwards*, I:13. Warfield reported that some 300 hundred converts were gathered in to the Northampton church during the first great awakening, and that more than 550 members were added to the church at Northampton during Edwards' pastorate. See Warfield, *Studies in Theology*, p. 524.

> mean by eloquence the power of presenting an
> important truth before an audience, with over-
> whelming weight of argument, and with such
> intenseness of feeling that the whole soul of the
> speaker is thrown into every part of the conception
> and delivery; so that the solemn attention of the
> whole audience is riveted, from the beginning to
> the close, and impressions are left that cannot be
> effaced; Mr. Edwards was the most eloquent man I
> ever heard speak.[39]

As far as the style of preaching of Jonathan Edwards is
concerned, it is a common notion that he laboriously read
every word of his sermons. This, however, is not the
case. It is true that the majority of the extant manuscripts
of Edwards's sermons are those which are written out in
full. But there are numerous sermons which are in outline form. Likely, Samuel Hopkins correctly averred that
even with the sermons which were written out in full,
there was a freedom from dependence on the manuscript.
Hence, Edwards "read most that he wrote: still he was
not confined to them; and if some thoughts were suggested to him while he was preaching, which did not occur to him when writing, and appeared pertinent, he
would deliver them with as great propriety and fluency,
and often with greater pathos, and attended with a more
sensibly good effect on his hearers, than what he had
written." And with the sermons which were presented
in outline form, he would have necessarily spoken from
those outlines, using them as somewhat of a springboard
for further elucidation of his thoughts.[40]

In a sermon on John 5:35, Edwards taught:

> It is the excellency of a minister of the gospel to be
> both a burning and shining light. . . . If a minister

---

[39] Edwards, *Works*, I:cxc.
[40] Cited in Murray, *Jonathan Edwards: A New Biography*, p. 190.

has light without heat, and entertains his auditory
with learned discourses, without a savor of the
power of godliness, or an appearance of fervency, of
spirit, and zeal for God and the good of souls, he
may gratify itching ears, and fill the heads of his
people with empty notions; but it will not be very
likely to reach their hearts or save their souls. And
if, on the other hand, he be driven on with a fierce
and intemperate zeal, and vehement heat, without
light, he will be likely to kindle the like unhallowed
flame in his people, and to fire their corrupt pas-
sions and affections; but will make them never the
better, nor lead them a step toward heaven, but
drive them apace the other way. . . . But if he ap-
proves himself in his ministry as both a burning and
shining light, this will be the way to promote true
Christianity amongst his people, and to make them
both wise and good, and cause religion to flourish
among them in the purity and beauty of it.

In 1737, Edwards's own personal documentary of the
first great awakening was published as *A Faithful
Narrative of the Surprising Work of God in the Conversion of
Many Hundred Souls in Northampton, and the Neighboring
Towns and Villages.* In this work the author, as historian,
tells of the positive changes, as evidence of genuine conversion, which occurred in the lives of many members of
his congregation. This work of God was not restricted to
Northampton, but spread up and down the Connecticut
River Valley. In *Faithful Narrative*, Jonathan Edwards
not only speaks to and commends the good works of a
genuine conversion, but he also condemns the excesses of
religious fervor which were present in the New England
revivals. He also condemned the Arminianism of his day,
which he saw as a threat to true Christianity.

Regarding the frenetic excesses, Edwards wrote: "An
intemperate, imprudent zeal, and a degree of enthusiasm
[frenetic religious fervor], soon crept in and mingled it-

self with that revival of religion; and so great and general an awakening being quite a new thing in the land, at least as to all the living inhabitants of it, neither the people nor ministers had learned thoroughly to distinguish between solid religion and its delusive counterfeits."[41] Doubtless, Edwards would have been in full agreement with his friend George Whitefield, who summarized the matter:

> Though it is the quintessence of enthusiasm to pre-
> tend to be guided by the Spirit without the written
> Word, yet it is every Christian's bound duty to be
> guided by the Spirit in conjunction with the writ-
> ten Word of God. Watch, therefore, I pray you, O
> believers, the motions of God's blessed Spirit in
> your souls, and always try the suggestions or im-
> pressions that you may at any time feel by the
> unerring rule of God's most holy Word. And if they
> are not found to be agreeable to that, reject them as
> diabolical and delusive.[42]

After the fires of the first great awakening ebbed, there was a period of approximately five years before the second great awakening took place, beginning in 1740 and lasting until 1742. In this latter awakening, men such as George Whitefield and Gilbert Tennent were involved as itinerant preachers, along with Jonathan Edwards (also as itinerant). Here again, Edwards, as "America's keenest psychologist of Christian experience, probed the realities beneath the epiphenomena" in *Some Thoughts Concerning the Present Revival of Religion in New England.*[43]

---

[41] Edwards, *Works*, II:321..

[42] Cited in Murray, *Jonathan Edwards: A New Biography*, p. 248.

[43] Gerstner, *The Rational Biblical Theology of Jonathan Edwards*, I:15; see Edwards, *Works* (Yale), 4:289–530. Edwards was much opposed to men such as James Davenport, who stressed emotional extremism in conversion; but he did not deny that a real work of God was taking place even amongst the emotional awakening. "If this be not the

Further, Edwards preached a series of sermons during these years, which were later published in book form under the title of *A Treatise Concerning the Religious Affections*, generally considered to be one of the two greatest products of Edwards' pen; the other being *Freedom of the Will*. John Piper correctly claimed that

> This book is the mature, seasoned reflection of Edwards, and the most profound analysis of the difference between true and false Christian experience that emerged from the season of the great awakening. In fact, it is probably one of the most penetrating and heart-searching Biblical treatments ever written of the way God works in saving and sanctifying the human heart.[44]

It was in 1743 that Jonathan Edwards met the young missionary David Brainerd, who possessed an indefatigable zeal for the furtherance of Christ's kingdom among

---

work of God," he wrote, "I have all my religion to learn over again, and know not what use to make of the Bible" (*Works* [Yale], 16:97).

[44] Piper, *God's Passion for His Glory*, p. 59. It is sometimes mistakenly understood that when Jonathan Edwards speaks of "affections" that he is speaking of mere "emotions." But this is not so. Rather, as explained by N. R. Needham, for Edwards, the affections are "a strong response of the will to what the intellect sees—whether that response is desire, hope, joy, love, pity, grief, fear, anger, or hatred" (*The Experience That Counts*, p. 11). Or as stated by Edwards, the affections are "no other than the more vigorous and sensible exercises of the inclination and will of the soul. . . . The will, and the affections of the soul, are not two faculties: the affections are not essentially distinct from the will, nor do they differ from the mere actings of the will and inclination of the soul, but only in the liveliness and sensibleness of exercise." See Jonathan Edwards, *Works* (Yale), 2:96-97. It is also obvious from these statements that Jonathan Edwards did not fall into the trap of faculty psychology, claiming that the mind, will, and emotions are separate faculties of the one human person. Rather, to Edwards, the mind, will, and emotions are all separate functions of the one human person.

the Indians. "There appeared to be nothing of any considerable importance to me," wrote Brainerd, "but holiness of heart and life, and the conversion of the heathen
to God."[45] There was an immediate bond established
between these two evangelists.

In the spring of 1747, Brainerd, dying of tuberculosis,
came to live in the Edwards home. There he was cared
for by Edwards's seventeen-year-old daughter, Jerusha.
David Brainerd died in the fall of that year at the age of
twenty-nine. Edwards preached his funeral service:
"True Saints When Absent from the Body Are Present
with the Lord." Jerusha died some five months later in
the winter of 1748, and was buried next to David
Brainerd. Her gravestone bears the text of Psalm 17:15: "I
shall be satisfied when I awake in Thy likeness."
Concerning Jerusha, Edwards lamented:

> Since this, it has pleased a holy and sovereign God
> to take away this my dear child by death, on the
> 14th of February, next following, after a short ill-
> ness of five days, in the 18th year of her age. She
> was a person of much the same spirit with Brainerd.
> She had constantly taken care of and attended him
> in this sickness, for nineteen weeks before his
> death; devoting herself to it with great delight, be-
> cause she looked on him as an eminent servant of
> Jesus Christ. . . . She had manifested a heart un-
> commonly devoted to God in the course of her life,
> many years before her death; and said on her death
> bed that she had not seen one minute, for several
> years, wherein she desired to live one minute
> longer, for the sake of any other good in life, but
> doing good, living to God, and doing what might be
> for His glory.[46]

---

[45] Cited in Murray, *Jonathan Edwards: A New Biography*, p. 302.
[46] Edwards, *Works* (Yale), 16:241.

Jonathan Edwards considered David Brainerd to be such an example of God-centered living that he wrote *An Account of the Life of the Late Reverend Mr. David Brainerd.* "Edwards was so impressed with David Brainerd," wrote George Claghorn, "that he resolved to write his biography. Brainerd's exemplary life embodied ideals he admired: doctrine fidelity, missionary zeal, vital religious experience, indomitable courage in overcoming obstacles, and radiant spirit."

The years of opposition in Edwards's life began in 1745. As noted earlier, Solomon Stoddard thought of the Lord's Supper as a "converting ordinance." Edwards became convinced that his venerable grandfather had erred. He wrote:

> My honored grandfather Stoddard, my predecessor in the ministry over this church, strenuously maintained the Lord's supper to be a converting ordinance, and urged all to come who were not of scandalous life, though they knew themselves to be unconverted. I formerly conformed to his practice, but I have had difficulties with respect to it, which have been long increasing, till I dared no longer to proceed in the former way.[47]

This being so, Jonathan Edwards was compelled to guard the Lord's table from what he saw as profanation. Unworthy members, then, under the policy established by Edwards, were not allowed to participate in the sacrament. In 1749 he wrote *An Humble Inquiry into the Rules of the Word of God Concerning the Qualifications Requisite to a Complete Standing and Full Communion in the Visible Christian Church*, with the purpose of showing from the Scriptures "that none ought to be admitted to the communion and privileges of members of the visible

---

[47] Edwards, *Works*, I:cv.

church of Christ in complete standing, but such as are in profession and in the eye of the church's Christian judgment, godly, or gracious [converted] persons."[48] Being opposed to Edwards' sview, the majority of the congregation was not even willing to read the treatise, and in 1750 the "male members voted ten to one that the greatest preacher ever to adorn an American pulpit be ignominiously dismissed."[49]

In his farewell sermon, from 2 Corinthians 1:14 ("As also you have acknowledged us in part, that we are your rejoicing, even as you also are ours in the day of the Lord Jesus"), Jonathan Edwards reminded his congregation that he had faithfully served them for a period of twenty-three years. He addressed the various groups within the congregation at the time: "Those who are professors of godliness," those "in a Christ-less state," "those who are under some awakenings," "the young people of the con-

---

[48] Edwards, *Works*, I:436. Some have misunderstood Jonathan Edwards on this point, averring that he envisioned an absolutely pure church, claiming that only those who are "genuine saints" are to be invited to the Lord's Supper. Even Charles Hodge seems to have been of this opinion with regard to Edwards's teaching on who is eligible to partake of the sacrament of the Lord's Supper (*Systematic Theology*, III:569–570). But this is a misrepresentation of his views. Rather, Edwards taught that "it is a credible profession and visibility of these things [godly actions], that is the church's rule in this case" (*Works*, I:434–435). Again, he wrote: "I am far from pretending to a discriminating judgment of men's spiritual state, so as infallibly to determine who are true converts and who are not, or imagining that I, or anybody else is sufficient for the execution of any such design as the setting up a pure church consisting only of true converts" (*Works* [Yale], 16:343).

[49] Gerstner, *The Rational Biblical Theology of Jonathan Edwards*, I:18. Sereno Dwight noted that the vote was 230 for dismissal and 23 against (cited in Gerald McDermott, *One Holy and Happy Society*, p. 168). Note is made that Edwards believed that only the male members of the congregation should vote (*Works* [Yale], 16:340). See Crampton and Bacon, *Built Upon the Rock*, p. 40.

gregation," and "the children of the congregation."
Appropriate words were spoken to each group. Edwards
told them, "I have spent the prime of my life and strength
in labors for your eternal welfare. . . . [I] have given
myself to the work of the ministry, laboring in it night
and day, rising early, and applying myself to this great
business to which Christ has appointed me." And he
exhorted and warned them, "You and I are now parting
one from another as to this world; let us labor that we
may not be parted after our meeting at the last day. . .
This is a sorrowful parting, but that would be more sorrowful." Then he reminded them that "God is the fountain of all blessing and prosperity, and He will be sought
to for His blessing." Finally, Edwards concluded:

> Having briefly mentioned these important articles
> of advice, nothing remains, but that I now take my
> leave of you, and bid you all, farewell; wishing and
> praying for your best prosperity. I would now com-
> mend your immortal souls to Him, who formerly
> committed them to me, expecting the day when I
> must meet you again before Him, who is the Judge
> of quick [living] and dead. I desire that I may never
> forget this people, who have been so long my spe-
> cial charge, and that I may never cease fervently to
> pray for your prosperity. May God bless you with a
> faithful pastor, one that is well acquainted with His
> mind and will, thoroughly warning sinners, wisely
> and skillfully searching professors [of Christ], and
> conducting you in the way to eternal blessedness.
> May you have truly a burning and shining light set
> up in this candlestick; and may you not only for a
> season, but during his whole life, that a long life, be
> willing to rejoice in his light. And let me be re-
> membered in the prayers of all God's people that
> are of a calm spirit, and are peaceable and faithful in
> Israel, of whatever opinion they may be with re-
> spect to terms of church communion. And let us all
> remember, and never forget our future solemn

> meeting on that great day of the Lord; the day of
> infallible decision, and of the everlasting and unal-
> terable sentence.[50]

At the time, Jonathan Edwards was forty-six years
old. He and Sarah still had nine children living at home.
He expressed some of his concerns in a letter written to a
friend shortly after the dismissal:

> I am now separated from the people between whom
> and me there was once the greatest union.
> Remarkable is the providence of God in this mat-
> ter. . . . I have now nothing visible to depend upon
> for my future usefulness, or the subsistence of my
> numerous family. But I hope we have an all-
> sufficient, faithful, covenant God to depend upon. I
> desire that I may ever submit to Him, walk humbly
> before Him, and put my trust wholly in Him. I de-
> sire, dear sir, your prayers for us, under our present
> circumstances.[51]

In the providence of God, even after the dismissal,
while the Northampton congregation was without a pastor, Edwards was requested to do the work of pulpit
supply on several occasions. Edwards did so with some
reluctance, but only for a week at a time.[52]

In December of 1750, the church in Stockbridge,
Massachusetts, asked Edwards to consider being their

---

[50] Edwards, *Works*, I:cc–ccvii.

[51] Edwards, *Works*, I:cxxii; Piper, *God's Passion for His Glory*, pp.
63–64.

[52] Edwards, *Works* (Yale), 16:359,364. George Claghorn noted that
during this same period of time, "After Edwards' dismissal from
Northampton, a small group of his former parishioners, numbering
about twenty families, adhered to him. Edwards frequently preached
to them in their homes." Some of the Northampton families that
sided with Edwards in the controversy over the Lord's Supper
desired that he become their pastor (*Works* [Yale], 16:367–368).

pastor. At the same time, he was asked by the Society in London for Propagating the Gospel in New England to evangelize the Housatonic Indians at Stockbridge, which was then a frontier village on the outskirts of New England. The congregation consisted of some white settlers and a number of Indians. Edwards spent that winter in Stockbridge, and accepted the call in the summer of 1751. The Edwards family moved to Stockbridge at that time.

There on the outskirts of New England, Jonathan Edwards once again faithfully gave himself to the ministry. He preached each Lord's Day, often through an interpreter.[53] While in Stockbridge, Jonathan Edwards wrote some of his weightiest and most influential treatises: *Freedom of the Will*,[54] *The Great Christian Doctrine of Original Sin Defended*, *The End for Which God Created the World*, and *The Nature of True Virtue*. Sereno Dwight referred to these as "four of the ablest and most valuable works which the church of Christ has in its possession." Here in Stockbridge, Edwards also worked on *The History of the Work of Redemption*, a work he had begun earlier. The years in Stockbridge, then, turned out to be some of the most productive of his life.

In 1757, Princeton College chose Jonathan Edwards to succeed Aaron Burr, Edwards's son-in-law, as its

[53] Edwards, *Works* (Yale), 16:451–452. Edwards wrote of his interpreter, John Wauwaumpequunnaunt, that he is "an extraordinary man on some accounts; understands English well, [is] a good teacher and writer and is an excellent interpreter. And perhaps there was never an Indian educated in America that exceeded him in knowledge, in divinity, [and] understanding of the Scriptures."
[54] Notably, Daniel Webster called *Freedom of the Will* "the greatest achievement of the human intellect." According to John Gerstner, *Freedom of the Will* set Arminianism back a full century. See Gerstner, *The Rational Biblical Theology of Jonathan Edwards*, I:19–20.

president upon Burr's death. He was reluctant to accept the position, believing that he could be of better service in Christ's kingdom by remaining in Stockbridge and completing writing projects which he had in mind.[55] In a letter which he wrote to the board, Edwards noted that his study and his writing "have long engaged and swallowed up my mind, and been the chief entertainment and delight of my life." Wrote Edwards: "So far as I myself am able to judge of what talents I have for benefiting my fellow creatures by word, I think I can write better than I can speak." Nevertheless, he agreed to seek counsel on the matter, and when that council concluded that he should accept the call to Princeton, Edwards did so, even with tears. He moved to Princeton, New Jersey, in January of 1758, intending to bring his family there in the spring of the following year.

One month after assuming the presidency at Princeton, Jonathan Edwards was inoculated for smallpox. The results were fatal. The pustules in his throat were swollen up to the point where he could not take fluids to fight off the fever. Knowing that he was dying, Edwards called his daughter Lucy (who was with him at Princeton at the time), and spoke to her the following:

> Dear Lucy, it seems to me to be the will of God that I must shortly leave you; therefore give my kindest love to my dear wife, and tell her that the uncommon union which has so long subsisted between us has been of such a nature as I trust is spiritual, and therefore will continue forever; and I hope she will be supported under so great a trial, and submit cheerfully to the will of God. And as to my children you are now to be left fatherless, which I

---

[55] These writing projects which he desired to complete included his own systematic theology, *A Rational Account of the Main Doctrines of the Christian Religion Attempted.*

> hope will be an inducement to you all to seek a
> Father who will never fail you.[56]

Shortly afterwards, Jonathan Edwards, ready to meet His God and Savior, looked around to those at his bedside and said, "Now where is Jesus of Nazareth, my true and never-failing Friend?" Then there was a moment of silence before he uttered these final words: "Trust in God, and you need not fear."[57]

Jonathan Edwards died on March 22, 1758. His doctor wrote a letter to Sarah Edwards, who was still living in Stockbridge, telling her of the demise of her husband.[58] Several weeks later, acknowleding the absolute sovereignty of God, Sarah wrote to her daughter Esther:

> My very dear child: What shall I say? A holy and good God has covered us with a dark cloud. O that we may kiss the rod, and lay our hands on our mouths! The Lord has done it, He has made me adore His goodness that we had him so long. But my God lives; and He has my heart. O what a legacy my husband, and your father, has left to us! We are all given to God; and that is where I am and love to be.[59]

On a rather inconspicuous gravestone in Princeton, New Jersey, the following words constitute Edwards's memorial:

---

[56] Edwards, *Works* (Yale), 16:5.

[57] Edwards, *Works*, I:clxxviii.

[58] According to Dr. William Shippen, the attending physician, and the one who had given Edwards the fatal smallpox inoculation, Edwards died with "freedom from pain" (Edwards, *Works* [Yale], 16:26).

[59] Edwards, *Works*, I:clxxix.

Would you know, oh traveler, what manner of person he was whose mortal parts lie here? A man indeed, in body tall yet graceful, attenuated through assiduity and abstinence and studies most intense; in the acuteness of his intellect, his sagacious judgment and his prudence second to none among mortals; in his knowledge of sciences and the liberal arts remarkable, in sacred criticism eminent, and a theologian distinguished without equal; an unconquered defender of the Christian faith and a preacher grave, solemn, discriminating; and by the favor of God most happy in the success and issue of his life. Illustrious in his piety, sedate in manners, but toward others friendly and benignant, he lived to be loved and venerated, and now, alas! to be lamented in his death. The bereaved college mourns for him, and the church mourns, but heaven rejoices to receive him. Go hence, oh traveler, and his pious footsteps follow.[60]

Jonathan Edwards the man is dead. Nevertheless, he continues to live today in his voluminous writings. There one can study under the Puritan sage himself. There one will come into contact with a man who was equally devoted to the truth as set forth in the Word of God, and to the God who set that truth forth for us in His Word. Jonathan Edwards was convinced that to know the truth is to know God, because He is the truth. "God is truth itself," he said.[61] Edwards believed and lived that

---

[60] Cited in Gerstner, *The Rational Biblical Theology of Jonathan Edwards*, I:19–20. After she arrived in Princeton, Sarah Edwards contracted dysentery and died on October 2, 1758. She is buried next to her husband in Princeton Cemetery (Nichols, *Jonathan Edwards: A Guided Tour of His Life and Thought*, p. 65).

[61] Jonathan Edwards, *Works* (Yale), 6:342. According to Jonathan Edwards, a love for the truth and a love for God are inseparable. God is the truth, and His Word is true. Further, this love for God "is the sum of all virtue" and it "tends to holy practice in the life." See Jonathan Edwards, *Charity and Its Fruits*, pp. 1–25 and 221–250.

which is taught in the Westminster Shorter Catechism
(Q. 1): "Man's chief end is to glorify God, and to enjoy
Him forever." In his own words: "By these things it appears that a truly virtuous mind, being as it were under
the sovereign dominion of love to God, does above all
things seek the glory of God, and makes this his supreme,
governing, and ultimate end."[62]

Along this same line, it is noteworthy that Jonathan
Edwards attempted to see all of the created world as a
reflection of the glory of God and His spiritual kingdom.
In Miscellany 362 he wrote:

> For indeed the whole outward creation, which is but
> the shadows of beings, is so made as to represent
> spiritual things. It might be demonstrated by the
> wonderful agreement in thousands of things, much
> of the same kind as in between the types of the Old
> Testament and their antitypes, and by spiritual
> things being so often and continually compared
> with them in the Word of God. And its agreeable to
> God's wisdom that it should be so, that the inferior
> and shadowy parts of His work should be made to
> represent those things that are more real and excel-

---

[62] Jonathan Edwards, *Works* (Yale), 8:559. It is precisely because
man's chief end is to glorify God and to enjoy Him forever that
Edwards correctly taught (contrary to the opinion of some) that
from a biblical standpoint it is not possible that a man should be
willing to be damned for the glory of God. In Miscellany 530 he
wrote: "It is impossible for any person to be willing to be perfectly
and finally miserable for God's sake, for this supposes love for God
is superior to self-love in the most general and extensive sense of
self-love, which enters into the nature of love to God. . . . Love to
God, if it be superior to any other principle, will make a man forever unwilling, utterly and finally, to be deprived of that part of his
happiness which he has in God's being blessed and glorified. . . .
The more a man loves God, the more unwilling will he be to be
deprived of this happiness." See John Piper, *Future Grace*, pp. 393–
394.

lent, spiritual and divine, to represent the things that immediately concern Himself and the highest parts of His work. Spiritual things are the crown and glory, the head and soul, the very end and Alpha and Omega of all other works: what therefore can be more agreeable to wisdom, than that they should be so made as to shadow them forth?[63]

In his book, *The Young Jonathan Edwards: A Reconstruction*, William Morris wrote that "genius must always fascinate; that is its character."[64] How true this was of our New England divine. The scholarly works of Edwards are of significant value for anyone who is concerned with learning and promoting the biblical truth of the Christian faith. One may not agree with all that Edwards ever penned, but a reading of his works will give a person knowledge of what this towering genius believed and taught; and he will be better off for so doing. For those things which Jonathan Edwards was concerned with and wrote about are ultimately matters of eternal consequence. Samuel Eliot Morison wrote:

---

[63] As we will see later, Jonathan Edwards was not suggesting here that general revelation is the equivalent of special revelation. Rather, it is that when he saw the objects of the physical world, it reminded him (so to speak) of the truth of the teaching we find in the Bible. Even as expressed in Miscellany 362, Edwards was fully of the opinion that all types, shadows, images, etc., must be derived from the teaching of the Word of God. And in his "Images of Divine Things," Edwards argued that he had biblical warrant for this kind of "typological" reasoning, while at the same time, he warned against giving way to a wild fancy in interpreting such types. Edwards believed that there is a medium between those who cry down all types, and those who are for turning all into nothing but allegory (*Works* [Yale], 11:53–58, 131–135, 148, 151). For more on this, see Wallace E. Anderson, *Works* (Yale), 11:3–33.

[64] Cited in McDermott, *One Holy and Happy Society*, p. viii.

Edwards might have been a naturalist or a great literary figure, but he chose theology because he believed that an exploration of the relation between
man and God was infinitely more important. He
would have considered our modern efforts to explore
outer space as of minor importance, since their objects are merely to extend human knowledge. He
looked beyond all stellar systems and galaxies, to
save men's souls for eternal life.[65]

---

[65] Cited in Murray, *Jonathan Edwards: A New Biography*, p. 58.

# 2

## *Jonathan Edwards on Knowledge*

In the preface to Jonathan Edwards' greatest work, *Freedom of the Will*, we read:

> Of all kinds of knowledge that we can ever obtain, the knowledge of God and the knowledge of ourselves, are the most important. As [the Christian] religion is the great business for which we are created, and on which our happiness depends; and as [the Christian] religion consists in an intercourse between ourselves and our Maker; and so has its foundation in God's nature and ours, and in the relation that God and we stand in to each other; therefore, a true knowledge of both must be necessary, in order to true religion.[1]

Without a knowledge of one's self, there is no knowledge of God. But to know one's self, God's image bearer, there must first be a knowledge of God. God, then, must be the first object of knowledge. And, according to Jonathan Edwards, the only way for one to come to this knowledge of God and self is by "the exploration of the heart, in light of Scripture." William Scheick, in *The Writings of Jonathan Edwards* (p. 132), said that this is what "provides the saint with the best intimation of divine reality."

Just like John Calvin and the Westminster Assembly before him, Jonathan Edwards began his theological and

---

[1] Edwards, *Works*, I:4.

philosophical enterprise with epistemology (the theory of knowledge).[2]

As already noted, from his voluminous writings it is evident that Edwards was a devotee of the Reformed principle of *sola Scriptura*, and the Westminster Confession of Faith (1:6):

> The whole counsel of God concerning all things necessary for His own glory, man's salvation, faith, and life, is either expressly set down in Scripture, or by good and necessary consequence may be deduced from Scripture: unto which nothing at any time is to be added, whether by new revelations of the Spirit, or traditions of men.

Jonathan Edwards believed that the indemonstrable axiom of Christian theology is that the Bible is the Word of God, and that it has a monopoly on truth. "Where is [there] any Word of God," he asked rhetorically in his sermon on 2 Timothy 3:16, "if it be not in the Bible?" Edwards, like Calvin before him, taught that the Scriptures are self-authenticating. "The Scriptures themselves," Edwards wrote in Miscellany 333, "are an evidence of their own divine authority."

According to Edwards (and the Westminster Assembly), the truth of Scripture is not restricted to the explicit statements of the Bible. Those things which can be logically deduced "by good and necessary consequence" are also God's truth. He wrote in Miscellany 426:

> And if what the Scripture says, together with what is plain to reason, leads [us] to believe any doctrine,

---

[2] Calvin, *Institutes*, I:1:1–3; *Westminster Confession of Faith*, chapter 1: "Of the Holy Scripture." Wallace Anderson is of the same opinion, that Edwards's starting point is epistemology; see Edwards, *Works* (Yale), 6:52–136.

> we are to look upon ourselves as taught this doctrine
> from Scripture. God may reveal things in Scripture
> which way He pleases; if by what He there reveals
> the thing in any way clearly discovered to the un-
> derstanding or eye of the mind, it is our duty to re-
> ceive it as His revelation.

Thus, David Brand properly commented that for Jonathan Edwards, theology was the "queen of the sciences," and "Holy Scriptures [are] the fountainhead of all human academic endeavor."[3] And Vincent Tomas wrote, Jonathan Edwards "took orders" from the Word of God alone.[4]

To be sure, there are apparent inconsistencies in Edwards's thought here. First, there is his empiricism. Empiricism, broadly defined, "is the doctrine that the source of all knowledge is to be found in experience."[5] But even though Jonathan Edwards did hold to a form of empiricism, agreeing to some degree that there is nothing in the mind which is not first in the senses, he did not believe that sensation produces any knowledge. Rather, it is God who immediately produces knowledge in the mind of all who receive knowledge.[6] In Miscellany 64,

---

[3] Brand, *Profile of the Last Puritan*, p. 146.

[4] Cited in Gerstner, *The Rational Biblical Theology of Jonathan Edwards*, I:116.

[5] W. L. Reese, editor, "Empiricism," *Dictionary of Philosophy and Religion*, p. 146. For more on the various methods of epistemology, see W. Gary Crampton, *The Scripturalism of Gordon H. Clark*, Part One, and W. Gary Crampton and Richard E. Bacon, *Toward a Christian Worldview*, chapter 2.

[6] Edwards, *Works* (Yale), 6:105–125. Also, Edwards denied what empiricists usually maintain, that is, that the mind of man is a *tabula rasa* (a "blank tablet") at birth or conception, i.e., it has no innate structure. As per his sermon on Romans 1:20 (and elsewhere), Edwards did teach that the mind has God-given innate propositional ideas from conception. Here, as well as in Miscellany 769 (and else-

he wrote: "Thus the matter is as to the Holy Spirit's gracious operations on the mind. We have shown in philosophy that all natural operations are done immediately by God only in harmony and proportion." And as he explained in his sermon on Matthew 16:17, when it comes to the divine light or the grace of salvific knowledge, here "there is such a thing as a spiritual and divine light, immediately imparted to the soul by God, of a different nature from any that is obtained by natural causes" (such as sensation). Further, as William Scheick pointed out, with spiritual maturation, Edwards progressively moved away from his earlier leanings toward empiricism.[7]

There is also the seeming inconsistency of Edwards's use of the theistic proofs. For example, in *Freedom of the Will*, he wrote:

> [T]he way that mankind comes to the knowledge of God is that which the apostle speaks of, Romans 1:20: "The invisible things of Him, from the creation of the world, are clearly seen; being understood by the things that are made; even His eternal power and Godhead." We first ascend, and prove *aposteriori;* or from effects, that there must be an eternal Cause; and then secondly, prove by argumentation, not intuition, that this Being must be necessarily existent; and then thirdly, from the proved necessity of His existence, we may descend, and prove many of His perfections *apriori.*[8]

---

where), we see that Edwards considered the infant in the womb as a (rational) human being.

[7] Scheick, *The Writings of Jonathan Edwards*, p. 32. Gerald McDermott is of the same opinion. According to McDermott, as Edwards matured in his thinking, he placed less emphasis on reason and more emphasis on Scripture. Thus, all of his reasoning was done in accordance with Scripture. (*Jonathan Edwards Confronts the Gods*, p. 60).

[8] Edwards, *Works*, I:16.

Yet, as Norman Fiering made clear, Edwards always made Holy Scripture the rule of judging all matters of the Christian faith, and not philosophical arguments. For example, in Miscellany 1337, he claimed that "the light of nature is in no sense whatsoever sufficient to discover this [Christian] religion." And in another place he said that apart from special revelation, "the very notion of such a Being [God] is all mystery, involving nothing but incomprehensible paradoxes, and seeming inconsistencies."[9] The same thought is expressed in his statement that "were it not for divine [special] revelation, I am persuaded, that there is not one doctrine of that which we call natural religion which, not withstanding all philosophy and learning, would not be forever involved in darkness, doubts, endless disputes, and dreadful confusion."[10] Even the "types" which the New England divine saw, not only in Scripture but in general revelation as well, were only able to be recognized "by those with a new sense of the heart [regeneration] and the Bible in their hands."[11] Edwards, said Fiering, is always setting forth his arguments from within the system of biblical Christianity, "within a dogmatic tradition." So, Edwards used philosophical arguments in an *ad hominem* fashion, to show the logical consistency of biblical theism, and the logical inconsistency of non-Christian thought.[12]

It seems that this is likely the case with the argument quoted above, where Edwards cites Romans 1:20 just

---

[9] Edwards, *Works*, II:483.

[10] Edwards, *Works*, II:462.

[11] McDermott, *Jonathan Edwards Confronts the Gods*, p. 112. For more on Edwards's typology, see Edwards, *Works* (Yale), volume 11. See also McDermott, *Jonathan Edwards Confronts the Gods*, pp. 110–129.

[12] Norman Fiering, *Jonathan Edwards's Moral Thought in Its British Context*, pp. 49ff.

prior to his statement about an *aposteriori* proof. That is to say, Edwards is merely showing that an effect necessarily needs a cause. And he bases his argument on Scripture (Romans 1:20), where he rests his case. As stated in Miscellany 1297, if men "are not led by [special] revelation and direct teaching into a right way of using their reason, in arguing from effects to causes, etc., they would forever remain in the most woeful doubt, and uncertainty concerning the nature and the very being of God."

With these things in mind, we see that Edwards's apparent inconsistencies with the *sola Scriptura* principle set forth in the Westminster Confession of Faith are not inconsistent at all. He may well have put too much emphasis on empiricism, and focused too much attention on philosophical arguments, at least in his early years. But at base, Jonathan Edwards held firmly to the principle of *sola Scriptura*. He "took orders" from the Word of God alone. He argued from the Bible, not to it. "For the New England divine," commented Stephen Stein, "the authority of the Bible was absolute."[13]

Gerald McDermott correctly stated that, like Calvin before him, Edwards believed that there is no true knowledge of God apart from Scripture. This is evident from one of his more extensive comments on how we know God and His works:

> Now there is nothing else that informs us what this scheme and design of God in His works is but only the holy Scriptures. Nothing else pretends to set in view the whole series of God's works of providence from beginning to end, and to show how all things were from God at first, and what end they are for, and how they are ordered from the beginning, and how they will proceed to the end of the world, and

---

[13] Stein, Introduction, Jonathan Edwards, *Works* (Yale), 15:33. Stein cites Peter Gay on this point.

what they will come to at last, and how then all things shall be to God. Nothing else but the Scriptures has any pretense for showing any manner of regular scheme or drift in those revolutions which God orders from age to age. Nothing else pretends to show what God would by the things that He has done and is doing and will do, what He seeks and intends by them. Nothing else pretends to show with any distinctness or certainty how the world began at first, or to tell us the original of things. Nothing but the Scriptures sets forth how God has governed the world from the beginning of the generations of men on the earth in an orderly history, and nothing else sets before us how He will govern it to the end by an orderly prophecy of future events, agreeable to the challenge that God makes to the gods and prophets and teachers of the heathen in Isaiah 41:22-23: "Let them bring forth, and show us what shall happen; let them show the former things, what they be, that we may consider them, and know the latter end of them; or declare us things to come. Show the things that are to come hereafter, that we may know that you are gods."[14]

## This author agrees with J. I. Packer:

It is clear from his [Edwards's] private notes and memoranda that metaphysical speculation fascinated him and was, indeed, his hobby, but he never let philosophy teach him his faith, or lead him away from the Bible. He philosophized from faith, not to it; he did not regard speculation as necessary to salvation, and no hint of his philosophical interests intrudes into his sermons. He took his convictions and concerns from the Bible, and it is as a Scriptural theologian that his true stature is to be measured.[15]

---

[14] Edwards, *Works* (Yale), 9:520–521.
[15] Packer, *A Quest for Godliness*, p. 315.

Further, Jonathan Edwards, as a Christian idealist, believed that the sum total of all truth exists in the mind of God. Nothing exists outside of the mind of God. Accordingly, if man is going to know the truth, he must come to know the eternal propositions in the mind of God. Some of these eternal propositional truths are implanted in man from conception by God. The mind of man is, as it were, enveloped by the mind of God, who enlightens man to understand the eternal propositions which are in His mind. So it is God alone who reveals truth to His image bearer, man. Moreover, taught Edwards, God has created human beings with rational minds that use the same laws of thought as His own. The principles of reason (logic) and knowledge are innately given by God to mankind. Thus, whenever human beings know truth, they know that which exists in the mind of God. They do not merely have a representation of the truth; they have the truth itself.[16]

This does not mean that Edwards believed that reason is the source of truth. Scripture is the source of truth. But there is perfect harmony between reason and biblical revelation, between Christianity and reason. In the Scriptures God has given us a rational revelation. There is, says the Confession (1:5), a "consent of all the parts." Christian man, then, is to reason from Scripture, not to it. "Revelation," claimed Edwards, "is given as a rule to reason."[17]

---

[16] Edwards, *Works* (Yale), 6:202–207, 332–393; Scheick, *The Writings of Jonathan Edwards*, p. 80; Sang Hyun Lee, *The Philosophical Theology of Jonathan Edwards*, pp. 58ff.

[17] Edwards, Miscellany 1340.

# 3

## *Jonathan Edwards on General and Special Revelation*

According to Jonathan Edwards, the God of the Bible is no *Deus absconditus* ("hidden God"). The triune God has revealed Himself to man in both general and special revelation, which are in harmony.[1] The former is general in audience (all mankind) and limited in content, whereas the latter, which is now found in Scripture alone, is more restricted in audience (those who read the Bible), and much more detailed in content. Due to its limited nature, general revelation must always be interpreted in light of special revelation: "The book of Scripture is the interpreter of the book of nature."[2]

Edwards taught that God has implanted an innate knowledge of Himself in all men. This knowledge, which includes the moral law of God,[3] is propositional and ineradicable. And this innate knowledge enables man to see

---

[1] Edwards, sermon on Romans 1:20; Jonathan Edwards, *Images or Shadows of Divine Things*, pp. 61, 70; Edwards, *Works* (Yale), 6:307–310. In the Edwardsean view, wrote Gerald McDermott, "Scripture and nature were finally harmonious in his system" (*Jonathan Edwards Confronts the Gods*, p. 128).

[2] Edwards, *Works* (Yale), 11:106.

[3] Edwards, sermon on Hosea 5:15. In Miscellany 533, Edwards used Romans 2:14–15 as a proof text regarding this innate knowledge of God possessed by all mankind.

43

the rich revelation of God in creation.[4] When man inter-
acts with God's creation, which demonstrates the attributes of God, man is, in some sense, forced "to think
God." The visible creation does not mediate knowledge
to man, for the visible universe does not set forth any
propositions (and knowledge can only be attained through
propositions). Rather, by way of "exciting ideas" (or rec-
ollection), it stimulates the mind of man, who as a rational
being is already in possession of *apriori* propositional information about God and His creation. This *apriori* information is immediately impressed upon man's consciousness. And it is God who does the "impressing." God
alone reveals truth to man.[5]

All men, therefore, have a knowledge of God, which
leaves them without excuse. But due to the noetic effects
of sin, fallen man continually suppresses the knowledge
of God which he has and knows to be true. General
revelation reveals God as Creator, but it does not reveal
Him as Savior. This being so, the propositional special
revelation of Scripture is necessary for man to come to a
sound and saving knowledge of God.[6] "The light of

---

[4] Edwards, Miscellany 119.

[5] Edwards, *Works* (Yale), 6:346, 361–370; Miscellanies 199–200, 267.
Along this same line of thought, Gordon Clark used the illustration
of a piece of paper on which is written a message in invisible ink.
The paper (by illustration, the mind) might appear blank, but in ac-
tuality it is not. When the heat of experience is applied to the mind
(as when heat is applied to the paper), the message becomes visible.
Human knowledge, then, is possible only because God has endowed
man with certain innate ideas. And those ideas are God's image.
Jonathan Edwards would have agreed with Clark. See Gordon H.
Clark, *Religion, Reason, and Revelation*, pp. 142–143.

[6] Edwards, sermon on Romans 1:20; *Works* II:51–57; Miscellany
1299. According to Edwards, general revelation, along with the earli-
est teachings of special revelation that God gave to Adam, is the reason for the basic religiosity of mankind and the many religions that
presently exist; see Miscellany 128 and *Works* II:253.

nature teaches that religion which is necessary to continue in the favor of God that made us," wrote Edwards, "but it cannot teach us that religion which is necessary to our being restored to the favor of God, after we have forfeited it."[7]

As the Westminster Confession of Faith (1:1) explains it:

> Although the light of nature and the works of creation and providence do so far manifest the goodness, wisdom, and power of God, as to leave men inexcusable; yet are they not sufficient to give that knowledge of God and of His will, which is necessary unto salvation. Therefore it pleased the Lord, at sundry times, and in divers manners, to reveal Himself, and to declare that His will unto His church; and afterwards, for the better preserving and propagating of the truth, and for the more sure establishment and comfort of the church against the corruption of the flesh, and the malice of Satan and of the world, to commit the same wholly unto writing: which makes the Holy Scripture to be most necessary; those former ways of God's revealing His will unto His people being now ceased.

Jonathan Edwards, along with the Westminster Assembly, concluded that due to the inadequacy of general revelation, it "plainly appears the necessity of divine [special] revelation."[8]

According to Edwards, the Scriptures are self-authenticating and self-evident. The Word of God, he wrote, does not "go about begging for its evidence, so much as some think; it has its highest and most proper evidence in itself."[9] The Scriptures themselves are an

---

[7] Edwards, *Works*, II:491.
[8] Edwards, *Works*, II:253.
[9] Edwards, *Works*, I:293.

evidence of their own divine authority. He also claimed that the Scriptures prove themselves by their own powerful light to be of divine authority. Again, he stated that what "God may reveal things in Scripture . . . it is our duty to receive it as His revelation," simply because it is the Word of God.[10]

Jonathan Edwards did not deny that there were a number of evidences that the Bible is the Word of God: "There are signatures of divine majesty to be seen in the Word, and signatures of divine wisdom and of divine holiness, and the evident marks of divine grace, that make it evident that the Word of God did proceed from a divine majesty and wisdom and holiness and grace."[11] Nor did he deny that these evidences are useful in the area of apologetics. As he stated, even though Scripture is self-evidencing and self-authenticating, still "great use may be made of external arguments, [and] they are not to be neglected, but highly prized and valued; for they may be greatly serviceable to awaken unbelievers, and bring them to serious consideration, and to confirm the faith of true saints."[12] But apart from the inner testimony of the Holy Spirit, taught Edwards, these evidences are vain. They cannot be sufficient. "It is impossible that men . . . should come at the force of arguments for the truth of Christianity." As cited above, if men, Edwards commented, "are not led by [special] revelation and direct teaching into a right way of using their reason, in arguing from effects to causes, etc., they would forever remain in the most woeful doubt, and uncertainty concerning the nature and the very being of God."[13] Edwards's doctrine is that of the Westminster Confession of Faith (1:4-5):

---

[10] Edwards, Miscellany 426.
[11] Edwards, sermon on Matthew 13:23.
[12] Edwards, *Works*, I:293.
[13] Edwards, Miscellany 1297.

> The authority of the Holy Scripture, for which it ought to be believed and obeyed, depends not upon the testimony of any man or church, but wholly upon God (who is truth itself) the author thereof; and therefore it is to be received, because it is the Word of God.
>
> We may be moved and induced by the testimony of the church to a high and reverend esteem of the Holy Scripture; and the heavenliness of the matter, the efficacy of the doctrine, the majesty of the style, the consent of all the parts, the scope of the whole (which is to give all glory to God), the full discovery it makes of the only way of man's salvation, the many other incomparable excellencies, and the entire perfection thereof, are arguments whereby it does abundantly evidence itself to be the Word of God; yet notwithstanding, our full persuasion and assurance of the infallible truth and divine authority thereof is from the inward work of the Holy Spirit bearing witness by and with the Word in our hearts.

Jonathan Edwards began his theological and philosophical study with epistemology. His starting point was divine, special revelation. Throughout his writings, he posited the infallible, inerrant Scriptures as foundational to all else. He operated out of a biblical cage.

# 4

## *Jonathan Edwards on Scripture*

From his early years, Jonathan Edwards devoted his life to the study of Scripture. Early on he resolved "To study the Scriptures so steadily, constantly, and frequently, as that I may find, and plainly perceive, myself to grow in the knowledge of the same."[1] Also, we have seen that he was an advocate of *sola Scriptura*, believing, as taught in the Confession (1:6), that "the whole counsel of God, concerning all things necessary for His own glory, man's salvation, faith, and life, is either expressly set down in Scripture, or by good and necessary consequence may be deduced from Scripture." Edwards's numerous writings fully attest to this fact. In the words of John Gerstner, "Jonathan Edwards's life . . . centered around the Bible." It was "the *sine qua non* of his rational Biblical theology."[2]

Moreover, we have seen that Edwards taught that Scripture is necessary for man to come to a sound and saving knowledge of God through Jesus Christ. And the Bible alone is to be considered as the sole source of truth and the authority by which man is to interpret all of life. The Bible is the standard by which all things are to be judged; nothing stands in judgment over the Word of God.

---

[1] Edwards, *Works*, I:xxi.
[2] Gerstner, *The Rational Biblical Theology of Jonathan Edwards*, I:140.

## Progressive Revelation

Jonathan Edwards, in the tradition of Reformed theologians throughout the centuries, held that biblical revelation was progressive in nature. In his *A History of the Work of Redemption*, which was originally set forth in a series of thirty sermon-lectures, he taught that there was a continuously enlarging body of special revelation from the time of Adam in the Garden of Eden to the time of the apostles. In Eden, God revealed Himself to Adam in propositional revelation, and He continued to do so until the close of the canon of Scripture. And throughout the entirety of the progress of revelation, the revelation is infallible and inerrant at every stage.

Jonathan Edwards, as a covenant theologian,[3] taught that one of the predominant ways that the progress of special revelation is recognizable in the Bible is in the various covenants that God has established with His church, in both the Old and New Testaments.[4] He taught that there is a unity that exists between the Old and the New Testaments, a unity which is founded upon the covenant of grace. It is "the unity of [redemptive] history," wherein we also see the unity of the Word of God.[5] As the Westminster Confession of Faith puts it (7:6): "There are not therefore two covenants of grace, differing in substance, but one and the same under vari-

---

[3] In his personal correspondence, Edwards criticized an early form of Dispensationalism (Works [Yale] 16:375–376).

[4] Bogue, *Jonathan Edwards and the Covenant of Grace*, pp.141–163. Jonathan Edwards agreed with the Westminster Confession of Faith (19:3; 25:1–2) that there is only one people of God in both the Old and New Testaments, and this is Christ's church. Old Testament Israel was the "church under age," and the church under the New Testament is the "church come of age." See Edwards, *Works* (Yale), 9:228–230, *passim*.

[5] Edwards, Miscellany 1353; sermon on Hebrews 13:8; sermon on Matthew 5:44.

ous dispensations."[6]

Jonathan Edwards maintained that when God created man (Adam), He entered into a "covenant of works" with him. In Edwards's words, "Perfect obedience is the condition of the first covenant."[7] If Adam had been obedient to God for a stipulated period of time, positive righteousness would have been imputed to him, and he would have been granted eternal life, along with his posterity: "If Adam our first surety had fulfilled the covenant made with him . . . then his posterity . . . would all have had the title to eternal life by virtue of the promises made to Adam their surety."[8] Adam, however, broke covenant with God; thus, he and his posterity fell from the state of original righteousness.[9]

Immediately subsequent to the Fall, God entered into

---

[6]  According to Stephen Stein, "Prophecy therefore allowed Edwards to organize the content of the entire Bible around Christ and to bind together the two testaments as coordinate witnesses to His work of redemption" (Cited in Edwards, *Works* [Yale], 11:159).

[7]  Edwards, Miscellany 786.

[8]  Edwards, Miscellany 1091.

[9]  Jonathan Edwards, *Works* (Yale), 3:344–345; sermon on Romans 6:14; sermon on Zechariah 4:7. See also Gerstner, *The Rational Biblical Theology of Jonathan Edwards*, II:94–97. It is noteworthy that for Edwards the immediate imputation of Adam's sin to his posterity is more "representational" or "realistic" than for most of those who hold to the view of immediate imputation. For Edwards, Adam's posterity was really there with him in the Garden of Eden; and they sinned as really as he did. There is "a constituted union of the branches with the root." "God, in each step of proceeding with Adam, in relation to the covenant [of works] . . . established with him, looked on his posterity as being one with him . . . . And though He dealt more immediately with Adam, yet it was as the head of the whole body, and the root of the whole tree. . . . From which it will follow that both guilt . . . and also depravity of heart, came upon Adam's posterity just as they came upon him, as much as if he and they had all co-existed, like a tree with many branches" (*Works* [Yale], 3:390, 389).

a new covenant with His elect: the covenant of grace. In this covenant, says the Confession (7:3): God "freely offers unto sinners life and salvation by Jesus Christ, requiring of them faith in Him, that they might be saved; and promising to give unto all those that are ordained unto life His Holy Spirit, to make them willing and able to believe." Edwards puts it this way:

> The first covenant failed of bringing men to the glory of God, through man's instability, whereby he failed of perseverance. Man's changeableness was the thing wherein it was weak through the flesh. But God had made a second covenant in mercy to fallen man, that in the way of this covenant he might be brought to the glory of God, which he failed of under the other. . . . Therefore God introduces another better covenant, committed not to his [Adam's] strength, but to the strength of one that was mighty and stable [Christ], and therefore is a sure and everlasting covenant. . . . The first was only to make way for the second.[10]

The covenant of grace, taught Edwards, was made with Christ, and with all of the elect in Him: "God makes the covenant [of grace] with Christ, the second Adam, for Himself and all His posterity."[11] This covenant was initially revealed in Genesis 3:15, with the first Messianic or gospel promise; that is, that God would send His Christ to redeem fallen elect sinners: "Presently upon this the gospel was first revealed on earth in . . . Genesis 3:15. . . . But these words of God in the fifteenth verse of the third chapter of Genesis were the first dawning of the light of the gospel after this darkness."[12] Moreover, said Edwards, this covenant promise

---

[10] Edwards, *Works*, II:599.
[11] Edwards, Miscellany 825.
[12] Edwards, *Works* (Yale), 9:132–133.

is that from which all the other biblical covenants flow: the Adamic, the Noahic, the Abrahamic, the Mosaic, the Davidic, and the New Covenant. With each covenant the body of redemptive, special revelation grew ("that gospel light which dawned immediately after the Fall of man gradually increases"), until consummated in the supreme and final revelation of God to man in the person and work of Jesus Christ.[13]

Yet even prior to the unfolding of the covenant of grace there was another supratemporal covenant. This covenant, which Edwards (and Reformed theology in general) refers to as the covenant of redemption, was an intra-Trinitarian covenant. This covenant, in a supralapsarian fashion, purposed the salvation of elect sinners by the person and work of Jesus Christ, their covenant representative. The covenant of redemption is the foundation of the covenant of grace; and the covenant of grace is the working out of the covenant of redemption.[14]

Special revelation in both the Old and New Testaments, then, is progressive and redemptive. And the New is superior to the Old, not so much in content or substance, as in administration and degree. The state of things under the Old Testament "was a typical state of things, and that not only the ceremonies of the law were typical, but that their [the Israelites'] history and constitution of the nation and their state and circumstances were typical. It was, as it were, a typical world."[15] Under the New Testament administration, this has changed. The Confession (7:5–6) teaches that, whereas the covenant under the Old Testament was administered by "promises, prophecies, sacrifices . . . and other types

---

[13] Edwards, *Works* (Yale), 9:127–386. The quote is from p.172.
[14] Edwards, *Works* (Yale) 9:117–119; Bogue, *Jonathan Edwards and the Covenant of Grace*, pp. 115–124.
[15] Edwards, *Works* (Yale), 11:146.

and ordinances delivered to the people of the Jews, all
fore-signifying Christ to come," under the New Testament administration, "Christ, the substance" has come;
and the covenant is now "held forth in more fullness,
evidence, and spiritual efficacy, to all nations, both Jews
and Gentiles," Edwards argued.

According to Edwards, the unity of special revelation
in both the Old and New Testaments is evident in a
number of ways. "Christ did not give to the world any
new moral precepts that were not either expressed or
implied in the precepts of the Old Testament and in the
Ten Commandments."[16] Moreover, both testaments, said
Edwards, have the same salvation, the same Mediator
(Jesus Christ)[17], the same method of justification by faith
alone in Christ alone, and the same application of Christ's
redemptive cross work by means of the Holy Spirit with
the Word of God. The two covenants differ only in
manner and circumstances. "The whole book, both Old
Testament and New, is filled up with the gospel, only
with this difference, that the Old Testament contains the
gospel under a veil, but the New contains it unveiled, so
that we may see the glory of the Lord with open face."[18]
"For though the covenant of grace indeed was in force
before His [Christ's] death," preached Edwards, "yet it
was of force no other wise than by His death."[19] This is
why this Puritan Sage referred to the covenant of grace as
"Christ's last will and testament."[20]

---

[16] Edwards, sermon on Matthew 5:44.

[17] In Miscellany 733, Edwards argued that "the Mediator ought to
be the middle person of the Trinity because, in being the Mediator
between the saints and God, He is the intermediate between the
Spirit and the Father, or between the third person and the first."
See also Miscellany 772.

[18] Edwards, *Works* (Yale), 9:290.

[19] Edwards, sermon on John 14:27.

[20] Edwards, sermon on Hebrews 9:15–16. Theologians debate the

## The Canon of Scripture

According to Reformed theology, the doctrine of progressive revelation maintains that the miraculous or charismatic word-gifts (e.g., tongues, prophecy) ceased at the end of the apostolic age, and the canon of Scripture was closed at that time. Because those former ways of God's revealing His will unto His people have now ceased, special revelation is now found in the 66 books of the Old and New Testaments alone. Now we find that "the whole counsel of God concerning all things necessary for His own glory, man's salvation, faith, and life, is either set down in Scripture, or by good and necessary consequence may be deduced from Scripture: unto which nothing at any time is to be added, whether by new revelations of the Spirit, or traditions of men."

John Gerstner notes that, even though Edwards nowhere lists the sixty-six books of the Protestant canon, there can be no doubt that he had the very list in mind which was enumerated by his favorite creed, the Westminster Confession. Said Edwards, agreeing with the Confession:

> God took this care with respect to the books of the Old Testament, that no books should be received by the Jewish church and delivered down in the canon of the Old Testament but what was His Word and owned by Christ. We may therefore conclude that He would still take the same care of His church

question of whether or not the Greek word *diatheke* should be translated "covenant" or "testament" in the New Testament. That is, is the primary focus on that of a covenant or of a last will and testament? Edwards was of the opinion that the word should be understood as "covenant," but always with the further understanding that the covenant of grace which God entered into with His elect people contains within it the need for the testamentary death of the Lord Jesus Christ, by which they inherit the blessing of eternal life (*Works* [Yale], 15:367).

with respect to the New Testament.[21]

According to Edwards, the charismatic word-gifts ceased no later than the end of the first century, when the Apostle John concluded the writing of the New Testament.[22] "These gifts," he wrote, "are not fruits of the Spirit that were given to be continued to the church throughout all ages. They were continued in the church, or at least were granted from time to time, though not without some considerable intermissions, from the beginning of the world till the close of the canon of the Scriptures was completed."[23] God speaks authoritatively now only in the Scriptures. There is no extra-biblical special revelation: "So that the canon of the Scriptures, that great and standing written rule that was begun about Moses' time, is now completed and settled, and a curse is denounced against him that adds anything to it or diminishes anything from it."[24] As Stephen Stein writes: "For Edwards, the boundaries of the Christian canon were not debatable. He accepted the prevailing view that the biblical canon had been closed long ago and that there was no need to augment it."[25]

According to Edwards, the cessation of the charismatic gifts is explicitly taught in 1 Corinthians 13:8–13. These gifts functioned as "childish things," and "they were adapted for the childish state of the church." They were a partial means of special revelation, and they are now supplanted by the perfect, complete Word of God, wherein we have "a perfect rule of faith and practice."[26]

---

[21] Edwards, Miscellany 1358.
[22] Edwards, *Works* (Yale), 9:365–369.
[23] Edwards, *Charity and Its Fruits*, p.310.
[24] Edwards, *Works* (Yale) 9:369–370.
[25] Stein, Introduction, in Edwards, *Works* (Yale), 15:5.
[26] Edwards, *Charity and Its Fruits*, pp. 304–322.

"The extraordinary influences of the Spirit of God im-
parting immediate revelations to men," he went on to say,
"were designed only for a temporary continuance while
the church was in its minority and never were intended
to be statedly upheld in the Christian church."[27]

## Inspiration

In a sermon on 2 Timothy 3:16 (and elsewhere),
Jonathan Edwards affirmed that the entirety of the Bible
(both the Old and New Testaments) is fully inspired by
God in the original manuscripts, and it has been "kept
[pure] all along" through the ages; "it has not  been
changed." It is "the verbally inspired and inerrant
Word."[28] It does not subjectively become the Word of
God, as in neo-orthodoxy.[29] Rather, "the Scripture is the
objective Word of God," given to mankind in logical,
propositional statements. Man was created in God's

---

[27] Edwards, sermon on 1 Corinthians 13:8–13.

[28] Edwards, sermon on 1 Corinthians 13:8–13.

[29]  Neo-orthodoxy maintains that parts of the Bible may
"subjectively" become the Word of God (different parts for different hearers at different times), but the Bible itself is not to be
considered "objectively" as the Word of God. Karl Barth and Emil
Brunner, for example, two twentieth-century neo-orthodox theologians, taught that the only true revelation of God to man is Jesus
Christ (the Word of God incarnate), and when Scripture "reveals"
Christ to the reader (the "Christ event"), then the Bible
"subjectively" becomes the Word of God to that individual.
According to neo-orthodoxy, it is beneath God, who is "wholly
other," to communicate the transcendental Christ through logical
propositions. Thus, God reveals events to us in the Bible, but not
the meaning of the events. The understanding of the meaning is a
subjective enterprise. Neo-orthodoxy, in claiming that revelation is
merely an event (i.e., something that happens), denies that the
Bible gives us propositional revelation. See Gordon H. Clark, *Karl
Barth's Theological Method*; and Robert L. Reymond, *Introductory
Studies in Contemporary Theology*, pp. 91ff.

image as a rational being, and God has given man a rational revelation in the Bible. Jonathan Edwards held to the Reformed doctrine of verbal, plenary inspiration. It is not merely the doctrine and/or the content of biblical revelation that is inspired; it is the Scripture itself. In the words of John Smith: "Edwards accepted totally the tradition established by the Reformers with respect to the absolute primacy and authority of the Bible, and he could approach the biblical writings with that conviction of their inerrancy and literal truth."[30]

Scripture, said Edwards, was written through God's prophets and apostles, who were moved along by the Holy Spirit so that they wrote nothing other than the infallible, inerrant Word of God: there was "an immediate inspiration that the prophets had when they were immediately inspired by the Spirit of God."[31] Commenting on 2 Peter 1:20, Edwards wrote that in the Scriptures, "it is not men's speaking their own sense of things or interpreting their own minds but the mind of God." It is God alone who speaks creatively in Scripture. The words of Scripture are the very words of God the Holy Spirit.

Jonathan Edwards did not hold to a mechanical and/or dictation theory of inspiration, wherein the human authors are to be seen as little more than stenographers.[32] Rather, he maintained that God the Holy Spirit acted upon the human authors in an "organic" way, in accordance with their own personalities, characters, tempera-

---

[30] Cited in Sproul, Gerstner, and Lindsley, *Classical Apologetics*, p.243.

[31] Edwards, Miscellany 20.

[32] Jonathan Edwards frequently used the word "dictate" (and its cognates) in his writings. But this usage speaks to the result (i.e., the endproduct), not the mode, of inspiration. For Edwards, the words of Scripture could be no more the words of God the Holy Spirit than if they were literally dictated. See Gerstner, *The Rational Biblical Theology of Jonathan Edwards*, I:141–142.

ments, gifts, and talents. Each author wrote in his own style, and all the while it was the Holy Spirit moving him along to write infallible truth. The human authors were the penmen who wrote by the inspiration of the Spirit of God. For example, in Miscellany 303, Edwards spoke of Solomon, as the author of the Song of Songs, as follows:

> I imagine that Solomon when he wrote this song, being a very philosophical, musing man and a pious man, and of a very loving temper, set himself in his own musings to imagine and to point forth to himself a pure, virtuous, pious, and entire love, and represented the musings and feelings of his mind that in a philosophical and religious frame was carried away in a sort of transport, and in that his musings and the train of his imaginations were guided and led on by the Spirit of God. Solomon in his wisdom and great experience had learned the vanity of all other love than of such a sort of one. God's Spirit made us of his loving inclination, joined with his musing philosophical disposition, and so directed and conducted it in this train of imagination as to represent the love that there is between Christ and His spouse.

Then too, speaking of Moses as an author of Scripture, Edwards wrote:

> Moses was so intimately conversant with God and so continually under the divine conduct, it cannot be thought that when he wrote the history of the creation and fall of man, and the history of the church from the creation, that he should not be under the divine direction in such an affair. Doubtless he wrote by God's direction, as we are informed that he wrote the law and the history of the Israelitish church.[33]

---

[33] Edwards, Miscellany 352.

Further, because the Bible is the infallible, inerrant Word of God, it is rational revelation. Scripture is logically consistent throughout. The alleged discrepancies in the Bible are just that, alleged, and nothing more.[34] Moreover, there are no contradictions or logical paradoxes in the Bible. There is no biblical assertion which is self-contradictory (or at least appears to be so), where one way or the other the assertion cannot possibly be reconciled before the bar of human reason. In Miscellany 139, he suggested "that there are many things in [the Christian] religion and the Scriptures that are made difficult on purpose to try men, and to exercise their faith and scrutiny, and to hinder the proud and self-sufficient." "Men are reasonable," preached Edwards, and "the Bible does not ask [them] to believe things against reason."[35] It is the non-Christian theories which are composed of "a whole heap of inconsistencies."[36]

## The Authority and Sufficiency of Scripture

Jonathan Edwards maintained that the full authority and the all-sufficiency of Scripture is due to its unique origin. The Bible is the Word of God, and it has a monopoly on truth. There is no other source of divine, special revelation. This is the Reformed principle of *sola Scriptura*. The 66 books of the Old and New Testaments

---

[34] Edwards, *Works*, II:676ff. Edwards was well-versed in the discipline of biblical criticism (lower criticism), as is evident in various of his writings. For example, in his "Notes on Scripture," he argued for the harmonization of the resurrection accounts of the four evangelists (*Works* [Yale], 15:154–156); he affirmed, at length, the Mosaic authorship of the Pentateuch (*Works* [Yale], 15:423–469); and he also handled other seeming differences and seeming inconsistencies that are found in the Bible (*Works* [Yale], 15:146–147, 182–184).

[35] Edwards, sermon on Isaiah 3:10.

[36] Edwards, *Works*, I:30.

are all-sufficient, not only for man to come to a sound and saving knowledge of God, through Jesus Christ, but also to justify all knowledge and to interpret every area of life. Scripture is the sole authority by which all is to be judged. Nothing stands in judgment over the Word of God. Edwards, in accord with the prophet Isaiah, affirmed that our only rule in life is "the law and testimony." Said Edwards, "It was God's design, when He gave the church the Scriptures, so to make and dispose them, and to put so much into them, and in such a manner, that they should be completely sufficient of themselves, that they should hold forth to us things sufficient for us to know, and they should be sufficiently there exhibited, and that in all important matters, whether in doctrine or practice, the Scriptures should sufficiently explain themselves."[37]

In good Calvinistic tradition, Jonathan Edwards taught that the inner testimony of the Holy Spirit is necessary to corroborate the authority of the Word of God to fallen man. "From the Fall of man to our day," he commented, "the work of redemption in its effect has mainly been carried on by remarkable communications of the Spirit of God."[38] It is essential for man to have a knowledge of Scripture to be converted, but many men may have a sound knowledge of Scripture without being converted. Many non-believers have an understanding of the Scriptures, but without "the divine and supernatural light, immediately imparted to the soul by the Spirit of God," they never attain a spiritual understanding of the message of Scripture. There is a spiritual understanding of divine things which all natural and unregenerate men are destitute of. It is "only the Spirit [who] makes them

---

[37] Edwards, Miscellany 535.
[38] Edwards, *Works*, I:539.

see."[39] It is only the Word of God, as administered by the Spirit of God, which can subdue the heart of fallen man. In this process, however, the Spirit does not reveal any new information which causes the reader to believe. This spiritual light, said Edwards, is not the suggesting of any new truths or propositions not contained in the Word of God. Rather, the Spirit produces belief in the mind of the elect sinner so that he can and does believe.

According to John Gerstner:

> Edwards's theory of religious knowledge may be represented by the photographic developing process. When the picture is first taken on the emulsion, nothing appears or can be seen. When the film is developed the picture is seen. The developer adds nothing to the picture that is not already present, but it makes the picture visible. Natural men [nonbelievers] have a religious picture on their mind; they may have many such pictures; they may have many more than regenerate persons and, indeed, much better pictures. But not one of these fine pictures is ever developed. The divine and supernatural light [the Holy Spirit] is the developer God uses to make the beauty and sweetness of divine truth apparent to the regenerate.[40]

At the same time, said Edwards, the Holy Spirit is that member of the Godhead who further illuminates the teaching of Scripture for the believer. But again, in this process, the Spirit does not reveal any new information. Rather, the same Spirit progressively gives the Christian a greater understanding of the Scriptures. He sheds more light on the biblical texts so that the believer can more

---

[39] Edwards, sermon on 2 Corinthians 3:18.

[40] Gerstner, *The Rational Biblical Theology of Jonathan Edwards*, I:187. This is Jonathan Edwards's view of the "effectual call" (see the *Westminster Confession of Faith*, chapter 10).

fully grasp the teaching of the Word of God.

For this reason, Edwards stressed the importance of Bible study to his congregation. One cannot grow in the process of sanctification without a knowledge of the Word of God. "The most acceptable way of showing respect to Christ is to give hearty entertainment to the Word," preached Edwards in a sermon on Luke 10:38–42. Therefore, "every Christian should make a business of endeavoring to grow in knowledge of divinity [theology]. . . . Divinity comprehends all that is taught in the Scriptures, and so all that we need to know, or is to be known, concerning God and Jesus Christ, concerning our duty to God, and our happiness in God. . . . There is no other way by which any means of grace whatsoever can be of any benefit, but by knowledge. . . . Christians ought not to content themselves with such degrees of knowledge in divinity as they have already obtained. It should not satisfy them that they know as much as is absolutely necessary to salvation, but should seek to make progress . . . . However diligently we apply ourselves, there is room enough to increase our knowledge of divinity without coming to an end."[41]

In this sense, Scripture, along with the sacraments[42]

---

[41] Edwards, sermon on Hebrews 5:12.

[42] According to Jonathan Edwards, there are two New Testament sacraments: baptism and the Lord's Supper. Edwards did not hold to any form of an *ex opere operato* theory of the efficacy of the sacraments. He held to the view of paedobaptism and denied the view of paedocommunion (Gerstner, *The Rational Biblical Theology of Jonathan Edwards*, III:429–475). Edwards did not believe that all infants dying in infancy are saved; he did not believe that all those infants who were baptized as children of visible saints would be saved; nor did he believe that we can have absolute assurance that all such baptized infants of visible saints who die in infancy are saved (Miscellanies 577, 595, 816). Here he was in agreement with the Westminster Confession of Faith (10:3; 28:4). He also concurred with the Confession (28:3), that "dipping of the person into the

and prayer, functions as a "means of grace." According to the Westminster Shorter Catechism (Q. 88), the means of grace are "The outward and ordinary means whereby Christ communicates to us the benefits of redemption, [and they] are His ordinances, especially the Word, sacraments, and prayer; all which are made effectual to the elect for salvation." Edwards, agreeing, taught that these means are indispensable to the sanctification of the Christian. "God's Spirit," he wrote, "always attends His ordinances."[43] "All the stated means of grace," he taught, were established "in the apostolic age . . . and are to remain unaltered to the day of judgment."[44] God's kingdom advances on earth (individually and corporately), he said, not by extraordinary means, but by the preaching of the gospel, and the use of the ordinary means of grace. The Spirit conveys knowledge to the elect through the Word of God preached and studied, and through the sacraments as explained and understood by the Word. This is the reason Edwards advocated a weekly administration of the Lord's supper.[45]

Edwards, being the "pure Puritan" that he was, stressed the importance of preaching, for in preaching there is the impressing of divine things on the heart and affections of the hearers. As stated by Irvonwy Morgan:

> The essential thing in understanding the Puritans

---

water is not necessary: but baptism is rightly administered by pouring or sprinkling water upon the person." In fact, said Edwards, "baptism by sprinkling" (or "pouring") is "a more lively representation of the thing signified by baptism than dipping or plunging" (Miscellany 694).

[43] Edwards, *Works*, I:539.

[44] Edwards, *Works* (Yale), 9:364–370. The quote is from p.370.

[45] Edwards, *Works*, I:cxxiii. According to Edwards, it was nothing other than "Christ's institution" that called for "the administration of the Lord's Supper every Lord's day" (*Works* [Yale], 16:366).

was that they were preachers before they were anything else . . . what bound them together, under-
girded their striving, and gave them the dynamic to
persist was their consciousness that they were called
to preach the gospel.[46]

Here, once again, Jonathan Edwards was exemplary.
Not only was he a master theologian and philosopher,
"but for virtually his entire adult life Edwards was first
and foremost a preacher."[47] And he was a preacher par
excellence. In John Gerstner's analysis:

Jonathan Edwards was, in my opinion, the greatest
preacher, from the standpoint of content of his
messages, who has appeared in history since apostolic times. . . . From the standpoint of deep and
solid exegesis, clear and profound articulation of
doctrine, searching, thorough, and fervent evangelistic application, I have never found Edwards's
equal. This [was] a preacher extraordinary of the
Word of God.[48]

As cited earlier, this is also the verdict of that gentle-
man who was asked by Sereno Dwight whether or not
Edwards was an eloquent speaker:

He [Edwards] had no studied varieties of the voice,
and no strong emphasis. He scarcely gestured, or
even moved, and he made no attempt by the ele-
gance of his style, or the beauty of his pictures, to
gratify the taste, and fascinate the imagination. But,
if you mean by eloquence, the power of presenting
an important truth before an audience, with over-

[46] Irvonwy Morgan, *The Godly Preachers of the Elizabethan Church*, p. 11.
[47] Eds., Edwards, *A Jonathan Edwards Reader*, p. xvi.
[48] Gerstner, *The Rational Biblical Theology of Jonathan Edwards*, I:480.

whelming weight of argument, and with such intenseness of feeling, that the whole soul of the speaker is thrown into every part of the conception and delivery; so that the solemn attention of the whole audience is riveted, from the beginning to the close, and impressions are left that cannot be effaced; Mr. Edwards was the most eloquent man I ever heard speak.[49]

Along this same line, commenting on the pastoral ministry of Jonathan Edwards, J. I. Packer wrote: "All his life he labored, fearlessly and tirelessly, to understand and apply the Bible. . . . All his life he fed his soul on the Bible; and all his life he fed his flock on the Bible . . . . As a Bible-lover, a Calvinist, a teacher of heart religion," Jonathan Edwards, being a "pure Puritan, indeed one of the purest and greatest of all the Puritans," was "a gospel preacher of unction and power."[50]

When it came to preaching the Word of God, Jonathan Edwards, like the Apostle Paul before him, "was innocent of the blood of all men," for he did not shun to declare to his hearers the whole counsel of God (Acts 20:26–27). "Ministers are not to preach those things which their own wisdom or reason suggests, but the things that are already dictated to them by the superior wisdom and knowledge of God." Further, ministers of the gospel must not "reject any doctrine that is taught by divine revelation." God "holds them [accountable] to go and preach that Word."[51] According to Jonathan Edwards, it is the excellency of a minister of the gospel to be both a burning and a shining light. And "it is the duty of ministers of the gospel, in the work of their ministry, to follow the example of their great Lord and Master

[49] Edwards, *Works*, I:cxc.
[50] Packer, *A Quest for Godliness*, pp. 310, 314.
[51] Edwards, sermon on 1 Corinthians 2:11–13.

[Jesus Christ]."⁵²

As an evangelist, Edwards did not hesitate to warn his hearers that, apart from Christ, they were "sinners in the hands of an angry God." "He that does not believe on the Lord Jesus Christ," preached Edwards, "the wrath of God abides on him."⁵³ But "when those that have been earnestly seeking Christ come to find Him, they have reason to rejoice with exceeding great joy."⁵⁴ There are, however, those "that have seeming come to Christ that do not love Christ above their dearest earthly enjoyments; they are not Christ's disciples."⁵⁵ "That which distinguishes the profitable hearers of God's Word from all others is that they [spiritually] understand it and bring forth the fruit of it."⁵⁶

"God's Word always comes as conqueror," said Edwards; "those that are not conquered by conversion shall be conquered by destruction and the execution of its threatenings."⁵⁷ Indeed, he preached, there is a great difference between converted and unconverted men. Those who come to savingly believe in Christ, however, must never think that it is of their own doing. Rather, the grace of salvation is the work of God alone: it is a divine and supernatural light immediately imparted to the soul by the Spirit of God. It is God who "exercises His sovereignty in the eternal salvation of men."⁵⁸

---

⁵² Edwards, sermon on John 13:5–15.
⁵³ Edwards, sermon on John 3:36.
⁵⁴ Edwards, sermon on Matthew 2:10.
⁵⁵ Edwards, sermon on Luke 14:26.
⁵⁶ Edwards, sermon on Matthew 13:23.
⁵⁷ Edwards, *Works* (Yale), 5:105.
⁵⁸ Edwards, sermon on Romans 9:18.

## The Law of God

Reformed theology does not separate the law and the gospel, though each is carefully distinguished from the other. Jonathan Edwards was of this same mind. Law without gospel is merely a dead letter. But there is no gospel without the law, which reveals one's sinful nature and his need for the grace of God in the person and work of Christ. Here the law of God is exhibited to be as a school master to lead to Christ. The law, then, serves "as an instrument that the great Redeemer [Christ] makes use of to convince men of their sin and misery and helplessness and God's awful and tremendous majesty and justice as a lawgiver, and so to make men sensible of the necessity of Christ as a Savior."[59]

The moral law also functions as a pattern of life for the regenerate. It admonishes the Christian to seek God and obey His commandments. Here the law is not to be seen "as a covenant of works, but as a rule of life, so it is made use [of] by the Redeemer from that time [the giving of the law at Mount Sinai] to the end of the world as a directory to His people, to show them the way in which they must walk, as they would go to heaven. For a way of sincere and universal obedience to this law is the narrow way that leads to life."[60]

---

[59] Edwards, *Works* (Yale), 9:168; see also *Works* (Yale), 2:154–155.

[60] Edwards, *Works* (Yale), 9:169. Edwards is not teaching salvation by works here. He is clearly an advocate of justification by grace alone through faith alone in Christ alone (see his *Justification by Faith Alone*, published by Soli Deo Gloria Publications). What he is expressing here is the importance and necessity of good works which reveal that a genuine work of salvation has occurred in the individual. Saving faith will always be accompanied by good works. See Ephesians 2:8–10 and the *Westminster Confession of Faith* (11:2): "Faith, thus receiving and resting on Christ and His righteousness, is the alone instrument of justification; yet it is not alone in the person justified, but is ever accompanied with all other saving

Jonathan Edwards distinguished the three traditional categories of the law of God: moral, judicial (civil), and ceremonial. Agreeing with chapter 19 of the Westminster Confession, he taught that the moral law, which comprises the Ten Commandments and the "general equity" of the judicial law which God gave to Israel as a nation, is continually binding on men and nations. He was of the opinion, for example, that the civil magistrate is obliged to uphold God's law in its function as God's minister. "Magistrates," as well as ministers of the gospel, and "every living soul, [are] now obliged to arise and acknowledge God in this work" for promoting His kingdom.[61] The same argument is found in *Charity and Its Fruits*, where Edwards contended that "it will dispose magistrates to act as the fathers of the commonwealth with that care and concern for the public good which the father of a family has for his household." This includes the magistrate's responsibility to execute murderers, in accordance with God's law: "God established it as a rule, henceforward to be observed, that murder shall be revenged in a course of public justice."[62]

---

graces, and is no dead faith, but works by love."

[61] Edwards, *Works*, I:389. Edwards demonstrated his concurrence with the teaching of the Westminster Confession of Faith (23:3): "yet he [the civil magistrate] has authority, and it is his duty, to take order, that unity and peace be preserved in the church, that the truth of God be kept pure and entire; [and] that all blasphemies and heresies be suppressed," in his support of the decision in the Robert Breck affair. Breck (1713–1784) was accused of heresy (he taught that the Scriptures are not fully inspired, and that the heathen may well be saved without Christ) by the ministers of Massachusetts in 1735, and sentenced to jail by the civil magistrate. For Edwards's approval of this decision, see *Works* (Yale), 12:4–17, 91–163. Then too, in Miscellany 1012, he taught that the judicial law of Moses had been (correctly) adopted by other nations in one form or another.

[62] Edwards, *Works* (Yale), 15:328–329.

Jonathan Edwards, as with Calvin before him, considered the work of the civil magistrate to be of great importance. In a sermon on Ezekiel 19:12, he preached that civil rulers are "strong rods" within a community. God tells us that there is a "need of government in societies." God has ordained that good rulers are "vehicles of good to mankind." Scripture even refers to these leaders as "gods." The magistracy is a great and important business. And men serving in this capacity should do so as God commands in His law. They are "heads, princes or governors, to whom honor, subjection and obedience should be paid."[63]

As far as the ceremonial law is concerned, it was given to Israel as a "typical law." These laws "prescribed the ceremonies and circumstances of the Jewish worship and their ecclesiastical state"; they are no longer binding.[64] These "things of the Old Testament are types of things appertaining to the Messiah, His kingdom, His salvation made manifest from the Old Testament itself."[65] "When Christ died, then there was an end to those types and shadows, because they were then all fulfilled."[66] Edwards, then, was in complete agreement with the Westminster Confession (19:3):

> God was pleased to give to the people of Israel, as a church under age, ceremonial laws, containing sev-

---

[63] Edwards, Miscellany 336. McDermott wrote that Edwards held to a Republican form of government (*One Holy and Happy Society*, pp. 137, 155, 157, 176). Edwards also taught that in the (post-millennial) kingdom, that "a sort of theocracy should ensue." And that the "kings shall rather be as the judges were before Saul (which [republican form of; WGC] government was that which was best pleasing to God)" (*Works* [Yale], 5:136).

[64] Edwards, *Works* (Yale), 9:169; see also Miscellany 638.

[65] Edwards, Miscellany 1439.

[66] Edwards, *Works* (Yale), 15:325.

eral typical ordinances, partly of worship, prefiguring Christ, His graces, actions, sufferings, and benefits; and partly holding forth divers instructions of moral duties. All which ceremonial laws are now abrogated, under the New Testament.

Thus, we are to recognize that the elect of the Old Testament economy, which constituted the church "being in its minority," were saved in precisely the same way as those in the New. The elect realized that the ceremonial law pointed beyond itself to the coming Messiah[67]: "The Messiah, and the redemption which He was to work out by His obedience unto death, was the foundation of the salvation of all the posterity of fallen man, that ever were saved. . . . The saints of old trusted in the promises of a future redemption to be wrought out and completed by the Messiah, and built their comfort upon it."[68]

Summarizing Edwards's doctrine of Scripture, John Gerstner wrote:

> What shall we say? For him [Edwards] it [the Bible] was nothing other than the verbally inspired and inerrant Word, and he always, as Isaiah advised, "trembled" at His Word [Isaiah 66:2]. It had free course in him as he studied it day and night and preached it throughout his ministry. It was certified internally and confirmed by external credentials as well [as in the *Westminster Confession of Faith* (1:5)]. It was an "awful [awe-inspiring] book" with its dread warnings to the wicked and wondrous promises

---

[67] Edwards, *Works* (Yale), 11:307. According to Edwards, "All the people of Israel, if they exercised consideration, must suppose and understand that these things pertaining to the ceremonial law were appointed and used as representations and symbols of something spiritual, and not for the sake of any innate goodness in them or any value God had for them."

[68] Edwards, *Works* (Yale), I:287–288.

to the humble penitent. So Edwards, "boxed in" as he was by its authority, preached it in season and out of season [2 Timothy 4:2], laboring to make its unique and saving message plain and powerful while fully aware that no sinner in Northampton or anywhere would ever see and receive it as God's very Word until God Himself cast His divine and supernatural light upon its pages and its proclamation.[69]

---

[69] Gerstner, *The Rational Biblical Theology of Jonathan Edwards*, I:190.

# 5

## *Jonathan Edwards on God*

Gregg Singer once wrote that the doctrine of God ("theology proper") is central to the Calvinistic worldview "simply because it is central to the Scriptures which reveal Him." Calvinism "looks primarily to the glory of God as its focal point: man's chief end is to glorify God and to enjoy Him forever."[1] Certainly this was true with regard to the Calvinist Jonathan Edwards. "A deep sense of the beauty and excellency of God," claimed Stephen Nichols, "permeates all of Edwards's life and writings. It set his mind on fire and his heart aflame."[2] According to Edwards, God is infinitely exalted in gloriousness and excellency above all created things. He is the supreme Harmony of all. And "the end of the creation is that the creation might glorify [God]." Therefore, "the first effect of the power of God in the heart in regeneration is to give the heart a divine taste or sense; to cause it to have a relish of the loveliness and sweetness of the supreme excellency of the divine nature."[3]

Theologians normally divide the study of God into the being of God and the works of God. The former has to do with who God is; the latter studies what He does. We

---

[1] C. Gregg Singer, *John Calvin: His Roots and Fruits*, p. 11.

[2] Nichols, *Jonathan Edwards: A Guided Tour of His Life and Thought*, p. 21.

[3] Edwards, *Treatise on Grace*, published by Soli Deo Gloria as *Standing in Grace*.

will study Edwards's doctrine under the same rubric.

## The Being of God

Jonathan Edwards described God as follows: "God is infinitely, eternally, unchangeably, and independently glorious and perfect." In God there is "infinite power, wisdom, righteousness, goodness . . . [and] truth." He is the all-sufficient God, who "stands in no need of, cannot be profited by, or receive anything from the creature."[4] The triune God of Scripture, who is personal, is defined by our New England divine by means of His attributes. God is the totality of His attributes; He is identical with His attributes.

## The Attributes of God

Theologians often classify the attributes of God. Some utilize the headings of "absolute or immanent, and relative or transitive"; others use "greatness and goodness"; still others prefer "incommunicable and communicable." And some theologians do not find these classifications helpful at all. In his doctrine of theology proper, Edwards spoke of "two kinds of attributes of God"; they are "His natural attributes" and "His moral attributes."[5] The former (non-exhaustive list) includes God's infinity, eternality, aseity (self-existence), simplicity, immutability, truth, sovereignty, and omniscience. The latter (non-exhaustive list) includes God's holiness (which sums up the moral attributes), love, and justice. These comprise "the glorious attributes of God."

## Natural Attributes

*Infinity:* The God of the Bible, said Edwards in

---

[4] Edwards, *Works* (Yale), 8:428–429; Lee, *The Philosophical Theology of Jonathan Edwards*, p. 171.
[5] Jonathan Edwards, *The Religious Affections*, pp. 98–99.

various places, is "the supreme and infinite being." He is "necessary" Being. He is that "Being whose loveliness, honorableness, and authority are infinite." When we speak of God's infinity with regard to space, we refer to His omnipresence. "God is everywhere present with His all-seeing eye." "He is present by His knowledge and essence." God is "the Supreme Being" who "fills heaven and earth." But God is also distinct from His creation. He is infinite in His transcendence. He is not restricted by space and time. "God is infinitely exalted in gloriousness and excellency above all created beings." And there is an "infinite happiness" that exists between the persons of the Trinity.

*Eternality:* When we speak of God's infinity with regard to time, we refer to His eternality. God has always been and always will be. He "is eternal by the necessity of His own nature." With God there is "eternal duration, it being without succession, present, before, and after."[6]

*Aseity:* When we speak of God's aseity, we ascribe to Him independence and/or self-existence. God is underived and absolute. He depends on nothing or no one. According to Jonathan Edwards, commented Sang Lee, "creatures exist *per se* (by themselves or in themselves), while only God exists *a se* (not only in Himself but also from Himself)." With God there is an "absolute prior [to creation] actuality and aseity."[7] As expressed in His name, "I Am That I Am," God is completely independent and self-sufficient.[8] "God is the sum of all being."

*Simplicity:* There is an absolute unity in God. So much is this the case that we may say that "God and real existence are the same." Therefore, "we learn how properly it may be said that God is and that there is none else, and

---

6 Edwards, *Works*, II:496.

7 Lee, *The Philosophical Theology of Jonathan Edwards*, pp. 50, 204.

8 Edwards, *Works* (Yale), 6:345; *Works* (Yale), 8:461–463.

how proper are these names of the Deity: 'Jehovah,' and 'I Am That I Am.' "[9] The simplicity and/or unity of God, who is pure Spirit, also assures us that each and every one of God's attributes is identical with His being, as is the sum total of them.

*Immutability:* Edwards preached that the triune God is immutable. For Him to be able to change would deny His eternality. His plans and purposes, therefore, can never be altered, and He can do no evil. God's attribute of immutability also assures us that His promises can never fail: "God never fails in any instance of His faithfulness to the covenant engagements He has entered into in behalf of mankind."[10] The unchangeable nature of God does not mean, however, that He is a static being; rather, He is dynamic and active, working in His created order.

*Truth:* Truth, according to Edwards, is an attribute of God: "God is truth itself." This being so, we can be assured that His Word is true. Further, if we are to know the truth, we must know what is in the mind of God: "the consistency and agreement of our ideas [must agree] with the ideas of God."[11] And the fact that "God is truth itself" assures us that He has given us a rational revelation.

*Sovereignty:* "It is axiomatic in Edwards," wrote Sang Lee, "that God is the absolutely sovereign and eternal ground of all existence and creativity. . . . Supremely important for him was the principle of God's absolute sovereignty in all aspects of reality, both the material and the spiritual." The doctrine of God's sovereignty "remained for him a fundamental principle of all that he thought and wrote."[12] It is no wonder, then, that "it is

---

[9] Edwards, *Works* (Yale), 6:345.

[10] Edwards, sermon on Psalm 111:5.

[11] Edwards, *Works* (Yale), 6:341–342; sermon on 2 Timothy 3:16.

[12] Lee, *The Philosophical Theology of Jonathan Edwards*, pp. 8, 47–48.

sometimes remarked . . . that Edwards's doctrine of divine sovereignty was as exalted as any in the history of Christian thought."[13] In Edwards own words: "Absolute sovereignty is what I love to ascribe to God." The sovereignty of God includes His omnipotence. The sovereign God of Scripture is all-powerful; He is infinitely strong. Moreover, the all-powerful, sovereign God of Scripture has an eternal plan for the history of His created universe, and He governs and controls all within His creation to bring about His purpose. That is to say, "so vast was Edwards's sense of divine sovereignty that if God's consciousness ceased even for a moment, the universe itself would cease to be."[14] Indeed, the destiny of all men rests in the hands of almighty God: "The sovereignty of God is His absolute, independent right of disposing of all creatures according to His own pleasure."[15] "God does whatever He pleases," he preached in a sermon on Daniel 4:35.[16] And whatever He does is right, simply because He does it.

*Omniscience:* The triune God of the Bible, taught Edwards, is all-wise. He eternally knows all things completely and exhaustively. His knowledge of all things past, present, and future is all-comprehensive. Such knowledge renders the future certain and necessary, thereby ruling out all contingency.[17] God's is a perfect wisdom, a perfect knowledge, which is far above the wisdom of any creature. And whereas the knowledge possessed by the creature is discursive, temporal, and incomplete, God's knowledge is intuitive, original, time-

[13] McDermott, *One Holy and Happy Society*, p. 42.
[14] Eds., Edwards, in *A Jonathan Edwards Reader*, p. xii.
[15] Edwards, sermon on Romans 9:18.
[16] This sermon is published in the Soli Deo Gloria title *The Puritan Pulpit: Jonathan Edwards.*
[17] Edwards, *Works*, I:35–41.

less, and complete.[18] As noted, included in the attribute
of omniscience, is God's foreknowledge of all things. But
the biblical usage of God's foreknowledge, as found, for
example, in Romans 8:29, has reference to His sovereign
choice of the elect unto salvation: "God's eternal foreknowledge is the same with God's eternal election of
them [the elect] or choosing them from eternity to be
His."[19] And it is in the work of redemption that we see
the wisdom of God most clearly displayed.

**Moral Attributes**

According to Jonathan Edwards, the moral attributes
of God are more excellent, i.e., "more lovely" than the
natural attributes, because without the moral excellency
of God—the holiness of God—the natural attributes
would not be lovely at all. Omnipotence and omniscience by themselves do not make God a lovely, holy
being. But when the natural attributes are understood as
holy attributes, then they are lovely. Therefore, "a true
love to God for the beauty of His moral attributes necessarily causes delight for all His attributes; for His moral
attributes cannot be without His natural attributes.
Infinite holiness supposes infinite wisdom and infinite
greatness; and all the attributes of God, as it were, imply
one another."[20]

*Holiness:* Jonathan Edwards taught that the God of
Scripture is an infinitely holy God, who is incapable of
doing evil. And he defined the holiness of God as the
"excellency and beauty of God's nature whereby His
heart is disposed and delights in everything that is
morally good and excellent."[21] This is why the saints

---

[18] Edwards, Miscellany 74.
[19] Edwards, sermon on Romans 8:29–30.
[20] Edwards, *Works*, I:279.
[21] Edwards, sermon on Isaiah 6:3.

"love God in the first place because the beauty of His holiness or His moral perfection is supremely lovable in itself."[22] Certainly this was the case with Edwards himself, who commented that "the holiness of God has always appeared to me the most lovely of all His attributes."[23]

*Love:* The love of God is sometimes considered as the same thing as His holiness, wrote Edwards. And God's love for His creatures should be seen as two-fold: There is His love of benevolence and His love of complacency.[24] First, there is a love of benevolence, which is a creational love that extends to all of God's creatures. Even the ungodly have a share in this love of God: "God is kind to the unthankful and evil."[25] God promises many temporal blessings to the non-elect.[26] God's love of complacency, on the other hand, extends only to the elect. It is an everlasting love, which involves the redeeming cross work of Jesus Christ; and it is a mercy that could only be bestowed upon the elect by Him.[27]

Moreover, we are to understand that God loves infinitely. Thus, "there must have been an object from all eternity which God infinitely loves." And "the object which God infinitely loves must be infinitely, perfectly consenting . . . to Him; but that which infinitely and

---

[22] Edwards, *The Religious Affections*, p. 99.

[23] Edwards, *A Jonathan Edwards Reader*, p. 291.

[24] Edwards, sermon on 1 John 4:19. In his *Treatise on Grace*, Jonathan Edwards frequently refers to the distinction between common grace (which is a manifestation of God's love of benevolence to all creation) and saving grace (which is the manifestation of God's love of complacency to the elect).

[25] Edwards, sermon on Luke 6:35 in *The Puritan Pulpit: Jonathan Edwards*.

[26] Edwards, sermon on Philippians 4:19.

[27] Edwards, sermon on Romans 5:10, sermon on Jeremiah 31:3, and sermon on Philippians 4:19.

perfectly agrees is the very same essence." This, of course, is the self-love which eternally exists among the Trinity. And "the Holy Spirit is the act of God between the Father and the Son, infinitely loving and delighting in each other."[28]

*Justice:* The God of the Bible always acts with perfect justice and righteousness: "Nothing is more precisely according to the truth of things than divine justice; it weighs things in an even balance; it views and estimates things no otherwise than they are truly in their own nature."[29] The triune God is a just and righteous God. Thus, He has sworn that He will be revenged on wicked men. That is to say, God's attribute of justice includes His wrath against all evil. He hates evil and must punish it. The justice of God in the day of judgment "will appear strict, exact, awful, and terrible, and therefore [it will be] glorious."[30] Jonathan Edwards did not err as others have by stating that God hates the sin but loves the sinner. According to Edwards, God abhors persons for their sins. It is people that God sends to an everlasting hell, not their sins.

*Glory:* Jonathan Edwards frequently refers to the glory of God, which is associated with His attributes, both natural and moral. Sometimes the word "glory, as applied to God . . . signifies the communication of His fullness. Other times 'glory,' as applied to God in Scripture implies the view or knowledge of God's excellency." And, said Edwards, "it is manifest that God's name and His glory, at least very often, signify the same thing in Scripture."[31] Edwards would have agreed with Robert Reymond that "God's glory is the sum total of all of His

---

[28] Edwards, Miscellany 117, 94.

[29] Edwards, *A Jonathan Edwards Reader*, p. 226.

[30] Edwards, sermon on Mark 9:44.

[31] Edwards, *Works* (Yale), 8:518–523.

attributes as well as any one of His attributes." Or said
another way, God's glory is nothing other than "the in-
trinsic Godness of God."[32]

## The Trinity

The Westminster Shorter Catechism (Q. 5-6) teaches
that "there is but one only, the living and true God," and
that "there are three persons in the Godhead: the Father,
the Son, and the Holy Ghost; and these three are one
God, the same in substance, equal in power and glory."
Jonathan Edwards agreed; he averred that the one true
and living God of Scripture subsists in three persons:
Father, Son, and Holy Ghost, and all three members of
the Godhead are equally and eternally divine. Ontologically, "the persons of the Trinity are equal among
themselves."[33] In the Edwardsean view there is no room
for subordinationism nor modalism (or Sabellianism).
Subordinationism maintains that there is one God, who is
the Father. The Son and the Spirit are lesser deities, if
divine at all. Modalism, on the other hand, teaches that
God is one in essence and one in person. There are not
three persons in the Godhead, there are merely three
ways (modes) of referring to the one divine person.

Each of the three persons in the Godhead has distin-
guishing properties. The differences between the persons are not differences in essence; they are merely dis-
tinctions within the Trinity. That which distinguishes
the three members is the eternal paternity of the Father,
the eternal Sonship of the Son, and the eternal procession
of the Spirit.

This was Edwards's view: In Scripture we are taught
of "the [eternal] generation of the Son" and "the [eternal]

---

[32] Reymond, *A New Systematic Theology of the Christian Faith*, pp.
165-166.
[33] Edwards, Miscellany 402.

proceeding of the Holy Ghost."[34] But Edwards preferred to state this doctrine in a different manner. According to Edwards, the eternal begotteness of the Son consists in the Father's having a perfect idea of Himself, which is the Son: "The image of God which God infinitely loves and has His chief delight in is the perfect idea of God . . . [which is] the perfect idea of Himself." And the "Scriptures tell us that the Son of God is that image." Moreover, said Edwards, the Holy Spirit is that member of the Trinity who eternally proceeds from the Father and the Son in an act of divine and "infinite love and delight" that exists between them.[35] Again, he wrote: "God is glorified within Himself these two ways: 1) By appearing, or being manifested to Himself in His own perfect idea; or in the Son, who is the brightness of His glory; 2) By enjoying and delighting in Himself, by flowing forth in infinite love and delight towards Himself; or in His Holy Spirit."[36]

Or said more simply, for Jonathan Edwards, the Father has eternally been the Father, the Son has eternally been the Son, and the Holy Spirit has eternally been the Holy Spirit. Here we see a relational priority of the Father to the Son, and the Father and the Son to the Holy Spirit. But there is no essential difference. And all three members are ontologically divine, of one will and purpose.

In summation, Edwards wrote:

> And this I suppose to be the blessed Trinity that we read of in the Holy Scriptures. The Father is the Deity subsisting in the prime, unoriginated and most absolute manner, or the Deity in its direct

---

[34] Edwards, *Works* (Yale), 15:387.

[35] Edwards, Miscellany 94. See also Miscellanies 117 and 238.

[36] Edwards, Miscellany 448. See also Grosart, ed., *Selections from the Unpublished Writings of Jonathan Edwards*, p. 47.

existence. The Son is the Deity generated by God's understanding, or having an idea of Himself and subsisting in that idea. The Holy Ghost is the Deity subsisting in act, or the divine essence flowing out and breathed forth in God's infinite love to and delight in Himself. And I believe the whole divine essence does truly and distinctly subsist both in the divine idea and divine love, and that each of them are [sic] properly distinct persons.[37]

Edwards did, however, recognize an order of economy, or administration, within the Godhead. Here there is a form of subordinationism. But the subordination is not in the essence of the members of the Trinity, but in the function or role that each member has to perform in redemptive history: "Hence we may better understand the economy of the persons of the Trinity as it appears in the part that each one has in the affair of redemption."[38] This is the doctrine of the economic Trinity, which has to do with the works of God *ad extra* ("outside of Himself"). The *ad extra* works include creation and providence, which are for the purpose of redemption. It is God the Father who sent the Son into the world to accomplish the redemption of the elect. It is God the Father and God the Son who sent the Holy Spirit into the world to apply Christ's redemptive work to the elect. And there is always a perfect harmony that exists between the members of the Trinity. "All the persons of the Trinity do concur in all acts *ad extra*."[39]

---

[37] Edwards, "An Essay on the Trinity," *Treatise on Grace and Other Posthumously Published Writings*, p. 118.
[38] Edwards, "Treatise on Grace," Grosart, *Selections from the Unpublished Writings of Jonathan Edwards*, p. 49.
[39] Edwards, Miscellany 1062 and Miscellany 402.

## The Works of God

Reformed theologian Jonathan Edwards maintained that the works of God are determined by His decrees, and that these works can be summarized under the headings of creation and providence.

Edwards's view was that of the Westminster Shorter Catechism (Q. 7): "the decrees of God are, His eternal purpose, according to the counsel of His will, whereby, for His own glory, He has foreordained whatsoever comes to pass." In a sermon on Matthew 11:6, he preached that "God decrees all things from all eternity." And whatever God does, He does it for the manifestation of His own glory. According to Edwards, "all that is ever spoken of in Scripture as an ultimate end of God's works is included in the one phrase, the glory of God." So sovereign is God in His decretive will that all of the days of every man, woman, and child are both numbered and "precisely decreed to the hour, minute, second." And man "can do nothing to change it." "God unalterably determines the limit of men's life."[40]

Moreover, the sovereignty of God in His decretive purposes extends even to the Fall of man, and all other sins as well: "God has decreed every action of men, yea, [even] every action that is sinful and every circumstance of those actions." Sin "is foreordained in God's decrees, and ordered in providence. . . . God decrees all things, and even all sins."[41] Nothing falls outside of God's eternal decrees. This, of course, does not mean that God is the author of sin. He "orders" sin but does not "author" it.

In his *Freedom of the Will*, Edwards taught that the fact that God has eternally decreed the end of all things does not undermine the free moral choices of individuals, nor

---

[40] Edwards, sermon on Job 14:5.
[41] Edwards, *Works*, II:527–528, 534.

does it impinge upon the responsibility of man.
Nevertheless, the God of Scripture is the absolute
sovereign monarch of heaven and earth, who brooks no
competition.

When it comes to the decrees of God, Edwards's main
emphasis is on the eternal destiny of mankind. He
clearly endorsed the teaching of the Westminster
Confession (3:3), that "by the decree of God, for the
manifestation of His glory, some men and angels are
predestinated unto everlasting life, and others foreordained to everlasting punishment." God decrees, and
even delights in, the election of some and the damnation
of others; and He does so for His own glory.[42] In a
sermon on Romans 9:18, Edwards preached that God's
attribute of sovereignty necessitates "His absolute, independent right of disposing of all creatures according to
His own pleasure." Therefore, God has "mercy on
whom He will have mercy, and whom He will, He hard-
ens." It is not possible for reprobate man to be saved.[43]
Further, divine election and reprobation are not determined by God's foreknowledge of the thoughts or choices
of man: God's loving some and not others is antecedent to
any manner of difference in them. In fact, said Edwards,
the fact that God foreknows all things necessitates His
eternal decrees. It could not be otherwise. This is the
Reformed doctrine of double-predestination: God "has
absolutely determined who shall be saved and who shall
be damned."[44] Divine election necessitates divine
reprobation.

In accordance with classic Reformed orthodoxy,
Jonathan Edwards distinguished between God's decre-

---

[42] Edwards, *Works* (Yale), 8:503ff; sermon on 1 Peter 2:9; sermon
on Luke 16:23.
[43] Edwards, sermon on Matthew 13:23.
[44] Edwards, sermon on Matthew 11:6.

tive will and His preceptive will (as per Deuteronomy 29:29). The former determines all things that will ever occur. The latter, on the other hand, is revealed in God's Word, which men are enjoined to obey. The decretive will, said Edwards, is hidden in the mind of God, and it is absolute and determined by God alone. The preceptive will is that will of God for man which man is to live by. Man is accountable for the preceptive will, not the decretive will.

Thus, we are to understand that nothing in the universe occurs by chance. There are no contingent events; there is no such thing as luck or fate. All things that have ever taken place or that will ever take place occur as a result of God's sovereign decretive will; which will is the first cause and governing factor of all things.[45]

Edwardsean scholars are divided over the issue of his view of the logical order of the decrees. But this writer is of the opinion that Jonathan Edwards was a supra-lapsarian (*supra*, "above"; *lapsus*, "fall"). He taught that the logical order of the divine decrees finds the decree to elect and reprobate prior to, or above (*supra*), the decree to bring about the Fall (*lapsus*).[46] In the supralapsarian view, the purpose of creation is to glorify God the Father, through the glorification of God the Son, through the redemption of elect sinners (the church). In his "Blank Bible," for instance, Edwards wrote that "the creation of

[45] Edwards, Miscellany 818. This is why Jonathan Edwards followed the principle set forth in James 4:15 that we should never be presumptuous in the making of plans, formulating programs, etc., but always say "if the Lord wills," then I will do such and such. For example, in a letter to his father (March 24, 1757), Edwards wrote: "I intend, God willing, to be at Windsor some time near the beginning of June" (*Works* [Yale], 16:702).

[46] In the infralapsarian (*infra*, "below"; *lapsus*, "fall") view, the logical order of the divine decrees finds the decree to elect and reprobate after, or below (*infra*), the decree to bring about the Fall.

all things was with an aim and subordination to that great work of Christ as Mediator, viz. the work of redemption." In Miscellany 702, he argued that God's works of creation and providence are themselves subservient to the redemption of the church.[47] In Miscellany 710, he wrote that "the world was created that Christ might obtain a spouse." And in his *The End for Which God Created the World*, he frequently claimed that God created the world for the purpose that He might be glorified through the redemption of an elect people. John Wilson stated:

> In characteristic fashion, Edwards argued that while other divine activities, for example, in creating the world, might, strictly speaking, have preceded and been presupposed in that of redeeming humanity through time, redemption was in fact their purpose or final end. So he viewed the doctrine of providence as subordinate to that of redemption. Indeed, if redemption was superordinate to creation and providence, it stood as subordinate only to God's glorification.[48]

Jonathan Edwards's teaching on the decrees of God also gives us a biblical theodicy.[49]

The question of "theodicy" has to do with the justification of the goodness and righteousness of God in the face of evil in the world. The word, which supposedly was coined by the German philosopher Gottfried Leibniz (1646–1716), is derived from two Greek words (*theos*, God, and *dike*, justice). As it is manifestly clear that creation's *raison d'etre* is to serve the redemptive ends of

---

[47] In this same Miscellany (702), Edwards argues the supralapsarian view of the order of the decrees from Ephesians 3:9–11.

[48] John Wilson, Editor's Introduction, *A History of the Work of Redemption*, *Works* (Yale), 9:40–41.

God, it is logically consistent that the Fall of mankind must occur if God is to be ultimately glorified through the glorification of His Son, by means of the redemption of elect sinners. That is, God's foreordination of the Fall, and His providentially bringing it to pass (as taught by Edwards), are necessary.[50] He has purposed it for His own glory. Edwards believed that if Adam, in the covenant of works, had successfully passed his probation in the Garden of Eden, he would have been confirmed by God in positive righteousness; and his righteousness would have been imputed to all of his descendants (the entire human race). All mankind, then, would have gratefully looked to Adam, not to Christ, as the one who merited eternal life for them. For all eternity, God would then have to share His glory with His creature, Adam.[51] This, of course, could not be. The foreordained Fall must

---

[50] According to Edwards, "God gave our first parent [Adam] sufficient grace though He withheld an efficacious grace or a grace that should certainly uphold him in all temptations he could meet with" (Miscellany 436). God "withheld His confirming grace" (Miscellany 290). In other words, said Edwards, even in the Garden of Eden, Adam needed the efficacious grace of Christ to sustain him in the temptation.

[51] Edwards argued in Miscellany 809 that even if Adam, under the covenant of works, had obeyed God and merited salvation for himself and his posterity, the final locus of mankind would not have been heaven, but earth (i.e., not a new heaven and new earth, but a new earth). "Heaven is not a promise of the first covenant with Adam," wrote Edwards, "but is only the promise of the covenant of grace, and the inheritance which is alone purchased of Christ." The Apostle Paul makes this clear in 1 Corinthians 15, said Edwards. Adam, "the first man was of the earth, made of dust; the second Man [Christ] is the Lord from heaven. As was the man of dust, so also are those who are made of dust; and is the heavenly Man, so also are those who are heavenly. . . . Flesh and blood cannot inherit the kingdom of God" (verses 47–48, 50). The heavenly state belongs to Christ, the Man from heaven, and to all those who are in union with Him.

be viewed, as with all things, for the advancement of the glory of God: "God Glorified in Man's Dependence" is the title of Edwards' sermon on 1 Corinthians 1:29–31. The "redeemed are dependent on Him for all, and in every way." God's people will now be far more blessed because of the coming of Christ than they ever would have been blessed by an obedient Adam. This is why some of the Puritans even referred to the Genesis 3 event as "the fortunate Fall."

According to Edwards:

> [Man has] been brought to a state vastly better than its former being before the Fall. . . . So that hereby God acquires an infinitely great and strong right to the redeemed; for the right is equal to the expense that obtained it, since that expense was necessary, and the benefit of the redeemed equal to the expense; which is not only to the glory of God, but will be a matter of rejoicing to the redeemed, to think that God has so great a right to them, and will make [them], with so much the more earnestness of consent and desire, yield themselves to God, and devote themselves to serve and glorify Him.[52]

## Creation

God's works of creation and providence were determined by His eternal decrees. Jonathan Edwards agreed with the Shorter Catechism (Q. 9), that "the work of creation is God's making all things of nothing, by the word of His power, in the space of six days, and all very good." This does not mean, of course, that the world came out of nothing. Rather, argued Edwards, the creation came from the eternal propositions in the mind of God.[53] "Though these exercises of God [in creation]

---

[52] Edwards, Miscellany 508.
[53] Edwards, Miscellany 749. In this same miscellany, Edwards contended that the idea of self-creation, i.e., that the world created it-

. . . are in time. . . . They were always equally present in the divine mind."[54] Moreover, from writings such as Miscellany 984, it is evident that Edwards believed that God created the world out of no pre-existent material in a period of six solar days. That is, Scripture teaches us that the world is very young, and that "man is recent."[55]

The crowning act of creation, said Edwards, was the creation of man, the image-bearer of God. Man was created with both a non-physical and a physical aspect; he has both a body and a soul or spirit. The image of God rests (mainly) in the non-physical element of man. Man is a rational creature and herein is distinguished from the animals.

Then too, man, as created, possessed (and still possesses) a two-fold image of God: the natural image and the moral image. The former consists of "man's reason and understanding, his natural abilities, and dominion over creation." Man is a rational being. The latter, on the other hand, has to do with man's "holiness." The natural image of God in man is now defaced due to the Fall, but it is not effaced. Man still remains man. The moral image, however, was eradicated by the Fall, and can only be restored through the grace of God in Jesus Christ.[56]

---

self, is self-referentially absurd.

[54] Edwards, *Works*, I:102.

[55] Gerstner, *The Rational Biblical Theology of Jonathan Edwards*, II:237. Edwards's young earth theory is also evident in from his *A Humble Attempt*, where he wrote that the postmillennial kingdom of Christ ("that millennium that is described in Revelation 20") would not begin until (approximately) the year 2000, which he said would be the world's seventh millennium ("seventh thousand years"); see *Works* (Yale), 5:410, 394; also 129–130, 135. Jonathan Edwards was postmillennial in his eschatology (*Works* (Yale), 9:455–486). In Miscellany 827, he wrote against premillennialism.

[56] Edwards, *The Religious Affections*, pp. 98–99; sermon on Romans 7:14.

## Providence

"God determines whatsoever comes to pass,"
Edwards preached, "and orders all things by His providence." He often referred to God's works of providence.
One example is found in his *A History of the Work of
Redemption*, where he claimed that Ezekiel's wheels
(Ezekiel 1) are to be seen as "God's work of providence
through all ages." Moreover, this work of providence is
really one united plan, God's grand design, as He carries
out His work in redemptive history. Nothing can change
or overthrow the sovereign, providential work of God:

> Hence we may see what a consistent thing
> divine providence is. The consideration of what
> has been may greatly serve to show us the con-
> sistence, order, and beauty of God's works of
> providence. If we behold the events of provi-
> dence in any other view than that in which it
> has been set before us, it will all look like con-
> fusion, like a number of jumbled events coming
> to pass without any order or method, like the
> tossing of the waves of the sea. Things will look
> as though one confused revolution came to pass
> after another merely by blind chance, without
> any design or certain end.
>
> But if we consider the events of providence
> in the light in which they have been set before
> us under this doctrine in which the Scriptures
> set them before us, they appear far from being
> jumbled and confused, but an orderly series of
> events, all wisely ordered and directed in excel-
> lent harmony and consistence, tending all to
> one end. The wheels of providence are not
> turned round by blind chance, but they are full
> of eyes round about, as Ezekiel represents; and
> they are guided by the Spirit of God, where the
> Spirit goes they go. And all God's works of
> providence through all ages: they meet in one at
> last as so many lines meeting in one center.
>
> It is with God's work of providence as it is

the work of creation: it is but one work. The
events of providence be not so many distinct
independent works of providence, but they are
rather so many different parts of one work of
providence: it is all one work, one regular
scheme. God's works of providence be not dis-
united and jumbled, without connection or dependence. But all are united, just as the several
parts of one building: there are many stones,
many pieces of timber, but all are joined and
fitly framed together that they make but one
building. They have all but one foundation, and
are united at last in one topstone.[57]

But according to our New England divine, what the
Westminster Assembly refers to as "providence" should
more correctly be understood as God's continuing work
of creation. That is, not only did God create all things *ex
nihilo* at the first, but He continues to re-create all things,
thereby preserving and governing them.[58] John Gerstner
explained the Edwardsean teaching this way: "Created

---

[57] Edwards, *Works* (Yale), 9:121, 519–520. Edwards "chose the wheel
as the best representative of divine providence," as Gerald
McDermott explained, to "represent the return of all things to God
after their beginning in God." In this sense, "progress in the work
of redemption is ultimately circular" (*One Holy and Happy Society*,
p. 49). In Edwards's own words: "In the beginning of this revolution
all things come from God, and are formed out of chaos; and in the
end, all things shall return into a chaos again, and shall return to
God, so that He that is the Alpha will be the Omega" (*Works* [Yale],
5:54). See also Edwards's explanation in *Works* (Yale), 15:373–379.

[58] The doctrine of continuous creation, though not often taught today has been around for centuries. Jenson commented: "This doctrine has regularly appeared through Christian history, since it so
clearly is that of the Bible" (*America's Theologian*, p. 152). Other
Puritan theologians who held to the doctrine of continuous creation
are Richard Sibbes and William Ames. Cocceius also held this view
(See Gerstner, *The Rational Biblical Theology of Jonathan Edwards*,
II:190–191).

being of itself immediately falls into non-being and God must constantly recreate it to preserve it."[59] Wrote Edwards:

> Therefore the existence of created substances, in each successive moment, must be the effect of the immediate agency, will, and power of God . . . the existence of each created person and thing, at each moment of it, be from the immediate continued creation of God. It will certainly follow from these things, that God's preserving created things in being is perfectly equivalent to a continued creation, or to His creating those things out of nothing at each moment of their existence.[60]

The fact of God's providential control of all things should give the Christian the greatest comfort, the reason being, wrote Edwards in Miscellany 86, that "as Mediator [Jesus Christ] rules all events . . . so as to conduce to the good of His church, and to bring to pass the ends of His mediation." Elsewhere he wrote:

> The universe is the chariot in which God rides and makes progress towards the last end of all things on the wheels of His providence. . . . Therefore [Ezekiel 1:25–26] signifies as much as that God governs the whole world for the good of His church; the wheels of the chariot of the universe move for them, and the progress that God makes therein on His throne above the firmament, the pavement of His chariot, is for them, and every event in the universe is in subserviency to their help and benefit.[61]

---

[59] Gerstner, *The Rational Biblical Theology of Jonathan Edwards*, II:192.
[60] Edwards, *A Jonathan Edwards Reader*, pp. 240–241.
[61] Edwards, *Selections from the Unpublished Writings of Jonathan*

Edwards, then, concurred with Article 13 of the Belgic Confession:

> We believe that the same good God, after He had created all things, did not forsake them up to fortune or chance, but that He rules and governs them according to His holy will, so that nothing happens in this world without His appointment. . . . This doctrine affords us unspeakable consolation, since we are taught thereby nothing can befall us by chance, but by the direction of our most gracious and heavenly Father; who watches over us with a parental care, keeping all creatures so under His power that not a hair of our head (for they are all numbered), nor a sparrow can fall to the ground without the will of our Father, in whom we do entirely trust; being persuaded that He so restrains the devil and all our enemies that without His will and permission they cannot hurt us.

---

*Edwards*, pp. 99–100.

# 6

## *Jonathan Edwards on Christ*

Jonathan Edwards taught that the second person of the Godhead, Jesus Christ, is fully divine. He "is a divine person."[1] As the eternal Son of God, "Christ is the shining forth of the Father's glory."[2] But from the time of His incarnation, Jesus Christ is also fully human. He possesses both a human body and a human soul. Not only is He the Son of God, He is also the Son of man. He is both God and man. And being conceived in the womb of the virgin Mary by means of the Holy Spirit, He was without sin.[3]

Further, this New England divine maintained that there is a perfect hypostatic union which exists between the divine nature and the human nature of Christ in one person. And in this union, both natures remain distinct. Christ is fully God and fully man, yet one Lord Jesus Christ.[4] It is necessary that Christ be both fully God and fully man in order for Him to bridge the gap between God and man. As man, He could die an atoning death in behalf of His elect people; and as God He could give in-

---

[1] Edwards, sermon on Revelation 5:5–6.

[2] Edwards, sermon on Hebrews 1:3.

[3] Edwards, Miscellany 386.

[4] Edwards, sermon on Revelation 5:5–6; Miscellany 738. Note that Edwards opposed the kenotic doctrine, which teaches that, at the time of His incarnation, the second person of the Godhead laid aside some or all of His divine attributes. See Edwards, sermon on Revelation 5:5–6; sermon on Luke 22:44; Miscellany 513.

finite merit to the atonement.[5]

It is also noteworthy that, for Jonathan Edwards, all of life must be viewed as Christo-centric. As he clearly taught in his *History of the Work of Redemption,* Jesus Christ is the center of all things. Stephen Nichols explains:

> To be sure, Edwards offers us a philosophy of history in his *History of the Work of Redemption.* But, he also does a great deal more. He offers a helpful grid through which we can both fit together all of the pieces of Scripture and through which we can construct a cohesive theology. Grasping the big picture of God's plan of redemption helps us to make sense of all the details. Edwards also reminds us that there is a center that gives shape and meaning to life and to the world, that this center holds, and this center is Christ Himself.[6]

## Edwards on Christ and Soteriology

We have already seen that Jonathan Edwards taught that when God created Adam, He entered into a covenant of works with him wherein Adam acted as the federal head or representative of the entire human race. In this covenant, God promised eternal life to Adam and his posterity upon the condition of Adam's perfect, personal obedience to God's commands. Adam, however, disobeyed God. And when he fell, by virtue of the "constituted oneness or identity of Adam and his posterity in this affair,"[7] all mankind (with the exception of Christ, the second Adam) fell with him: "The beginning of the posterity of our first parents was after the Fall, for all his [Adam's] posterity by ordinary generation are partakers of

---

5 Edwards, *Miscellanies* 245, 350, 398, 772, 773, 846, 1214; sermon on Revelation 5:5–6.

6 Nichols, *Jonathan Edwards: A Guided Tour of His Life and Thought,* p. 156.

7 Edwards, *Works,* I:220.

the Fall and the corruption of nature that followed from it."[8]

All men, then, are judicially guilty in this first sin. Man is now in an ethical state of total depravity, unable to do anything that pleases God. He "stands in absolute need of a Redeemer."[9] "The nature of man is so corrupted that he is become a very evil and hurtful creature."[10] The "hearts of natural men are wholly corrupt, entirely destitute of anything spiritually good, not having the least spark of love to God."[11] Men are "polluted with sin; every step they take is attended with sin, so all the works that they do are polluted. They can perform no service, no business, but they contract their guilt and defilement, that they need the renewed washing of the blood of Christ."[12]

---

[8] Edwards, *Works* (Yale), 9:116. It is obvious from this statement, and from other of his writings, that Jonathan Edwards agreed with the Westminster Confession of Faith, that although judicial guilt was imputed to all mankind in Adam's sin, the pollution of sin is conveyed by means of natural generation. The Confession (6:3) reads: "They [Adam and Eve] being the root of all mankind, the guilt of this sin was imputed, and the same death in sin and corrupted nature conveyed, to all their posterity descending from them by ordinary generation." Interestingly, Edwards also taught that due to the fact that Jesus Christ was born of the virgin Mary, in a sinless state without a human father, we are to understand that the sin nature of mankind is conveyed by means of the male member of the marriage. Sin came into the world by the first male, Adam, and it continues to be propagated through the male (*Works* [Yale], 15:318–319).
[9] Edwards, Miscellany 814. See also Edwards, sermon on Matthew 11:16–19; and *Works*, I:182–187. Edwards taught that all false religions are as a result of the Fall of man in Genesis 3; they are all deviations, in some sort, from the one true religion of Biblical Christianity (Miscellany 307, 1255).
[10] Edwards, sermon on Matthew 10:17.
[11] Edwards, *Works* (Yale), 16:481.
[12] Edwards, *Works*, (Yale), 11:124.

Herein the Calvinist Edwards differed widely from his Arminian counterparts, who taught (and continue to teach) that, albeit man is a sinner in need of a Savior, he is capable of doing something to please God. Man does have the ability to "close with Christ." He is not in a state of "total depravity." But just because man does some outward good works on occasion, said Edwards, this does not mean that he is capable of doing that which pleases God: "It would be much more absurd to suppose that such a state of nature is not bad, under a notion of men doing more honest and kind things than evil ones, than to say, the state of that ship is good for crossing the Atlantic Ocean, though such as cannot hold together through the voyage, but will infallibly founder and sink, under a notion that it may probably go a great part of the way before it sinks, or that it will proceed and sail above water more hours than it will be in sinking"; or to insist "that the domestic [servant] of a prince was not a bad servant, because though sometimes he contemned and affronted his master to a great degree, yet he did not spit in his master's face so often as he performed acts of service." No, said Edwards, man "continually and progressively" sins because he is a sinner by nature.[13] And all of the outward good works of the unregenerate are nothing more than "splendid sins."[14]

As seen, immediately following the Fall of man, God entered into another covenant with elect man: the covenant of grace, which covenant itself is founded upon the intra-Trinitarian covenant of redemption. In the covenant of grace, which was first revealed in Genesis

---

[13] Edwards, *Works*, I:152–153.

[14] Edwards, Miscellany 965. Edwards here cites Augustine with approval. In Miscellany 797, Edwards referred to the "seeming virtues and good works" of the unregenerate as a "spurious brood," because such men are "bastards and not children."

3:15, Christ, as the federal head of God's elect, fulfilled the covenant of works on their behalf, and merited their salvation.[15] Furthermore, Edwards pointed out, there is only one covenant of grace for all ages. This being so, salvation is the same for those under the Old Testament administration as it is under the New.[16] Both Testaments, he taught, have the same salvation, the same Mediator (Jesus Christ), and the same method of justification by grace alone through faith alone in Christ alone. The two covenants differ only in manner and circumstances. Old Testament believers were saved, Edwards averred, by believing in Christ (even though under the name the "Angel of the Lord" or the "Messenger of the covenant"), just as are their New Testament counterparts. They all are aware that the Messiah was the Son of God. "The whole book, both Old Testament and New," he contended, "is filled up with the gospel, only with this difference, that the Old Testament contains the gospel under a veil, but the New contains it unveiled, so that we may see the glory of the Lord with open face."[17] Jesus Christ is "the Savior of the saints in all ages from the beginning of the world."[18] "It is most certain," he wrote, "both from Scripture and reason, that there must be a reception of Christ with the faculties of the soul in order to salvation by Him, and that in this reception there is a believing of what we are taught in the gospel concerning Him and salvation by Him, and that it must

---

[15] Edwards, *Works* [Yale], 9:117–119; *Works*, II:599; Miscellany 30; Miscellany 399.

[16] Edwards, sermon on Hebrews 13:8; sermon on Romans 6:14. Edwards also makes this plain in his "Types of the Messiah," wherein he showed that the Old Testament sacrifices all pointed beyond themselves to Christ as the true Savior (*Works*, II:671–674). The same is true with his sermon on Psalm 40:6–8.

[17] Edwards, *Works* (Yale), 11:228.

[18] Edwards, *Works* (Yale), 9:290.

be a consent of the will or an agreeableness between the disposition of the soul and those doctrines."[19] Thus,

---

[19] Edwards, Miscellany 27b. Later in this Miscellany, Edwards stated "that many of the ancient Jews before Christ were saved without the sensible exertions of those acts in that manner which is represented as necessary by some divines, because they had not those occasions nor were under circumstances that would draw them out; though without doubt they had the disposition, which alone is absolutely necessary now, and at all times and in all circumstances is equally necessary." To infer from this statement that Edwards did not believe that faith in Christ was necessary for some Old Testament Jews to be saved would be unfair. The first part of the Miscellany clearly states that "there must be a reception of Christ with the faculties of the soul in order to salvation by Him." And that the "disposition" that is necessary is a believing disposition, one that holds to the doctrines taught in Scripture about Christ. Then too, this would fly in the face of what Edwards has written elsewhere (as cited in the main text of this book), that belief in Christ is essential to saving faith. Likely, what Edwards is referring to is that under the Old Testament there was a lesser amount of revelation, and so believing Jews would necessarily have a lesser knowledge of the Messiah than those under the New Testament. Under the New Testament, with increased revelation, there is greater knowledge and greater responsibility. Certainly the Old Testament people of God could not have known Jesus Christ as Jesus, son of Joseph, as the New Testament saints do. But these Old Testament saints believed in accordance with the revelation given to them about Christ (they knew Him, for instance, as the "Angel of the Lord" and the "Messenger of the covenant"). And in this way, there was "a reception of Christ with the faculties of the soul in order to salvation by Him." These saints knew enough to be saved, and they possessed a believing disposition in the Messiah, and that is what was necessary for their salvation. See Miscellanies 663, 840, 884, 1283. In Miscellany 78, Edwards also spoke about elect infants dying in infancy who were saved based on the disposition that God had given them, even though they had not put their trust in Jesus Christ *per se*. Here again we see the New England divine's agreement with the Westminster Confession of Faith (10:3): "Elect infants, dying in infancy, are regenerated, and saved by Christ through the Spirit, who works when, and where, and how He

concluded Edwards, "the religion of the church of Israel was essentially the same religion with that of the Christian church," both being "built on the holy Scriptures."[20]

There can be little question that Jonathan Edwards was a Christian exclusivist.[21] He taught that Jesus Christ is the only Savior, and that it is essential for one to believe in Him in order to be saved. Even under the shadows of the Old Testament, it was always the second person of the Trinity who appeared to His people. And those who were saved put their trust in Him. Again, this does not mean that they knew as much about Christ as do New Testament believers; but they knew Christ. Even those in foreign lands who were saved were saved by believing in the Christ they had heard of through the special revelation brought to them by the people of God.[22] Even men like "Cornelius [Acts 10-11] did

---

pleases; so also, are all other elect persons who are incapable of being outwardly called by the ministry of the Word."

[20] Edwards, *Works* (Yale), 9:443.

[21] For more on "Christian Exclusivism," see W. Gary Crampton, *Christ the Mediator*, pp. 31–34.

[22] Edwards, *Works* (Yale), 15:369–372, 535–537. As with Augustine (*Retractions*, 1.12) before him, Edwards held to the *prisca theologia*, i.e., that "many religious truths" have been found in foreign lands, due to the propagation of Biblical teachings by God's people through the centuries (Miscellany 1351; see also Miscellany 986). He taught, for example, that subsequent to the flood Noah ruled China for many hundreds of years, thereby bringing God's special revelation to that land (Miscellany 350). To quote McDermott: "Edwards . . . filled hundreds of pages in his notebooks with evidence that the pagans had received knowledge about God the Redeemer [Jesus Christ] from the Jews and the *prisca theologia*. As far as he knew, the vast majority of the heathen had failed to take advantage of this knowledge, and so this knowledge was used for their condemnation rather than salvation" (*Jonathan Edwards Confronts the Gods*, 132–133). As seen, in Miscellany 965, Edwards taught that even the best acts of the unconverted pagans were

already in some respect believe in Christ even in the manner that the Old Testament saints were wont to do."[23]

We have also noted that for Edwards the salvation of the elect ultimately begins in God's eternal, supralapsarian plan. God, for His own glory and according to His own good purposes, eternally decrees the election of some and the reprobation of others: "God does exercise His sovereignty in the affair of men's eternal salvation."[24] Salvation, from beginning to end, is fully based on the divine initiative. Preached Edwards: "The things which God does for the salvation and blessedness of the saints are like an inviolable chain"[25] ; "God is the sole author of salvation of those that are saved even from the very first beginning of it in the eternal covenant of redemption even to the end and consummation of it in the eternal glory of the saints"[26]—and salvation is found in Christ alone.

---

nothing more than "splendid sins."
[23] Edwards, Miscellanies 663, 840, 884.
[24] Edwards, sermon on Romans 9:18.
[25] Edwards, sermon on Romans 8:29.
[26] Edwards, sermon on Hosea 13:9.

# 7

## *Jonathan Edwards on the Christian Experience*

Soteriology (from the Greek *soter*, savior) is the study of the work of redemption accomplished by Jesus Christ as it is applied to the elect. Although all three members of the Trinity are involved in the salvation of the elect, said Jonathan Edwards, it is the Holy Spirit who applies this grace. The Father elects, the Son redeems those whom the Father elects, and the Spirit applies Christ's redemptive work to the elect. Edwards preached, "God has provided a Savior for us and Christ has come and died." But, he went on, "the application of the redemption of the gospel [is] by the Holy Spirit [and] is of mere grace."[1] That is, "the work of the Holy Ghost as Christ's messenger is to convince men of sin, of righteousness, and of judgment."[2]

The salvation of the elect (both Old and New Testaments), then, has to do with their relationship with Christ. He is the federal head of His elect people. He is their representative, and they are in union with Him. This union with Christ, explained Edwards, is foundational to the entirety of the order of salvation. In Miscellany 1091 he wrote: "God the Father makes no covenant and enters into no treaty with fallen man distinctly by themselves. He will transact with them in such a

---

[1] Edwards, sermon on Zechariah 4:7.
[2] Edwards, sermon on John 16:8.

friendly way no other way than by and in [union with] Christ Jesus as members and as it were parts of Him."

And in another Miscellany, he wrote:

> Union with Christ. By virtue of the believer's union with Christ, he does really possess all things. . . . I'll tell you what I mean by possessing all things. I mean that God, three in one, all that He is, and all that He has, and all that He does, all that He has made or done, the whole universe, bodies and spirits, light, heaven, angels, men and devils, sun, moon, stars, land, sea, fish, fowls, all the silver and gold, kings and potentates, as well as mere men, are as much the Christian's as the money in his pocket, the clothes he wears, or the house he dwells in, as the victuals he eats; yea, more properly his, more advantageously, more his than if he commands all those things mentioned to be just in all respects as he pleased, at any time, by virtue of the union with Christ, because Christ who certainly does thus possess all things is entirely his, so that he possesses it all . . . only he has not the trouble of managing of it but Christ, to whom it is no trouble, manages it for him, a thousand times as much as to his advantage as he could himself, if he had the managing of all. . . . And who would desire to possess all things more than to have all things managed just according to his will.[3]

According to Jonathan Edwards, "this relation or union to Christ, whereby Christians are said to be in Christ . . . is the ground of their right to His benefits."[4]

Reformed theology teaches that there is a logical order (called the *ordo salutis*) which God has ordained, by

---

[3] Cited in Gerstner, *The Rational Biblical Theology of Jonathan Edwards*, III:222–223.

[4] Edwards, sermon on Romans 4:5.

which the application of redemption is applied to the elect, as well as the means thereunto. Says the Westminster Confession (3:6):

> As God has appointed the elect unto glory, so has He, by the eternal and most free purpose of His will, foreordained all the means thereunto. Wherefore they who are elected, being fallen in Adam, are redeemed by Christ; are effectually called unto faith in Christ by His Spirit working in due season; are justified, adopted, sanctified, and kept by His power through faith unto salvation. Neither are any other redeemed by Christ, effectually called, justified, adopted, sanctified, and saved, but the elect only.

Salvation is not to be seen as a one-step event. One is not converted and immediately glorified. Passages such as John 1:12–13, Romans 8:28–30, and Ephesians 1:3–14 and 2:8–10 teach us that there is a process involved. But even as we study the process, we must keep in mind that some of the parts of the *ordo salutis* may be synchronous, and the parts can in no way be separated. They are, said Edwards, like "strings in concert, if one is struck others sound with it."

Edwards never wrote out in systematic form an *ordo salutis*, but from a study of his various writings, the logical order of the application of redemption occurs as follows:

*Universal Call:* There is a "universal call" which goes out to all men who come under the hearing of the Word of God preached. This general call is "to sinners universally," inviting them to come to Christ for their salvation.[5] As noted earlier, Edwards taught that God's general revelation leaves all men without excuse. But special

---

[5] Edwards, sermon on Revelation 3:20; see also sermon on Genesis 3:23.

revelation is necessary for man to come to a sound and saving knowledge of God in Christ. Many of the philosophers of antiquity, claimed Edwards, may have had a large measure of non–saving grace given to them in their great mental capacity, but because they did not have the special revelation of the Word of God, they could not be saved.[6] Without the Word of God, there is no salvation possible. The heathen cannot be converted without it. Only those who come "under the call of the gospel" can be saved.[7] Hence, when there is a "famine" of the Word of God in a land, it is a disastrous thing, and a sign of God's judgment.[8]

*Seeking Salvation:* When the Word of God is preached, some hearers are hardened by it and reject it outright. Others are convicted of their sin by the gospel message and are "awakened" to their desperate state. They "are first awakened with a sense of their miserable condition by nature, the danger they are in of perishing eternally, and that it is of great importance to them that they speedily . . . get into a better state."[9] Still, however, these "awakened" sinners have not yet responded to the universal call of the gospel. What are they able to do? Jonathan Edwards told them to seek their salvation.

John Gerstner explained:

Probably the most distinctive thing about

---

[6] Edwards, sermon on Romans 14:7. Edwards, however, did not doubt that some "wise philosophers" could have received enough information about the Messiah that it may have been of "great benefit . . . to their own souls" (Miscellany 1162). This information would have come by the teaching of God's people as guided by the Holy Spirit. See the earlier note on Edwards's view of the *prisca theologia*.

[7] Edwards, sermon on Matthew 22:14.

[8] Edwards, sermon on Amos 8:11; sermon on Romans 1:24.

[9] Edwards, *Works* (Yale), 4:28.

Jonathan Edwards's evangelistic message is his
theory of seeking. A natural man could do certain things (use the means of grace, obey the
commandments of God outwardly, etc.) that
would probably issue in his salvation. This theory falls between the Arminian, on the one
hand, and the extreme Calvinistic, on the
other. According to the Arminian theory of salvation, the sinner was able of himself alone to
repent, believe, and be saved: all without the
working of regeneration having previously taken
place. According to Calvinism, regeneration
must precede such gracious acts as believing and
repenting. When the message comes to the unconverted he has no ability to receive it savingly
unless God, at the same time the message is
given, works faith in the person. He will then
evince this regeneration by believing the gospel
which is presented. But if God does not work
faith, there is nothing, according to some
Calvinists, that the sinner can do. At this point
perhaps the Calvinist Edwards is distinct
(though certainly not among Puritans). He in-
sists that there is something that the sinner can
do; in that, he agrees with the Arminians. Still,
he denies with vigor that the sinner can do what
the Arminian thinks he can do. But at the same
time he disagrees with those Calvinists who say
that there is nothing that the sinner can do.
According to Edwards, he can do something
non-saving but promising and hopeful: seek.[10]

Edwards was not the first to teach this doctrine.
Calvin, commenting on Luke 13:23–24, had earlier said
that Christ directs all men to "strive to enter by the narrow gate," revealing that those who would enter in to
eternal life must take measure to do so. But it was the

---

[10] Gerstner, *Jonathan Edwards, Evangelist,* pp. 191–192.

Puritans,[11] and particularly Edwards and his grandfather Solomon Stoddard, who more fully developed the doctrine of "seeking salvation."

Man, taught Edwards, prior to regeneration, is in a state of total depravity, unable to do anything that pleases God. He "stands in absolute need of a Redeemer." Apart from the grace of God, he will perish in his sin. But even though he has no spiritual ability to "close with Christ," the "awakened" sinner, being under conviction, being aware of his spiritual condition, and being concerned about it, does have the natural ability to do those things which *may* indeed lead to his salvation. That is, whereas only the regenerate man has the spiritual ability to seek God, the unregenerate still has the natural ability to seek salvation, though not God. The unregenerate man can and should go to church, where he will hear the gospel preached. He can and should read the Bible. He can and should cry out to God for mercy. He can and should talk to his pastor and other Christians about his need for a Savior, asking them to pray for his salvation. None of these acts of "seeking" will merit the lost sinner anything before God. But God may use these "means" to draw the sinner savingly to Christ. For certain, said Edwards, and his grandfather before him, "a possibility of being saved is much to be preferred to a certainty of perishing."[12]

"It is true," said Edwards, that "men never will be disposed to use the means [or grace] unless they are

---

[11] John Gerstner lists William Perkins, John Preston, and Thomas Hooker as other Puritans who taught the doctrine of "seeking salvation" (*The Rational Biblical Theology of Jonathan Edwards*, III:54). See also Erroll Hulse, *Who Are the Puritans?*, 158–160. Hulse wrote of the Puritan's teaching on "Preparation on the way to salvation." Edwards's grandfather, Solomon Stoddard, wrote what Dr. Gerstner called "the finest manual on Reformed evangelism ever written": *A Guide to Christ*, which was on seeking salvation.

[12] Edwards, sermon on 2 Kings 7:3–4.

awakened . . . but that does not argue that the using the means is not in their [natural] power."[13] The "seeking sinner" must realize that "persons ought to do what they can for their salvation."[14] They must know that "God stands ready to forgive every sinner upon his hearty confessing and forsaking sin."[15] And "if we truly come to God for mercy, the greatness of our sin will be no impediment to pardon." To be sure, God does not "make any promises of success to unregenerated seekers of salvation." Yet, there is a greater probability that those who seek their salvation will indeed be converted, because "we know that God's manner is to bestow His grace on men by outwards means; otherwise, to what purpose is the Bible, and sabbath, and preaching, and sacraments, or doctrinal knowledge of religion?"[16]

*Effectual Call:* The universal call is not efficacious. According to our New England divine, it is not possible for a person to come to a saving knowledge of God without sound doctrine, but sound doctrine itself is not enough.[17] It is only when the Holy Spirit applies the Word to the elect sinner's heart that the call of God becomes effectual: "Whatever in the work of redemption is done immediately or upon men's souls is the work of the Spirit." And "the work of the Holy Ghost [is] to make men understand the way of sinners' reconciliation and acceptance with God through Christ." He is the one who

---

[13] Edwards, sermon on Ecclesiastes 4:5.
[14] Edwards, sermon on Ecclesiastes 9:10.
[15] Edwards, sermon on Proverbs 28:13.
[16] Edwards, Miscellany 538.
[17] Edwards, sermon on Matthew 13:23. Even the devil, taught Edwards, is sound in his theology. He "has undoubtedly a great degree of speculative [theoretical or conjectural] knowledge in divinity; having been, as it were, educated in the best divinity school in the universe, viz., the heaven of heaven" (*Works*, II:43).

gives divine light into the heart of converts.[18] There is no new revelation given in this work of the Spirit; there are no new propositions revealed to the elect sinner. The Spirit merely opens his heart to understand the teachings of Scripture. "The first act of the Spirit of God," wrote Edwards in Miscellany 397, "is in spiritual understanding or in the sense of the mind, its perception of glory and excellency, etc.—in the ideas it has of divine things."

*Regeneration:* Although regeneration and effectual calling stand in the closest possible relationship, there is a difference in the two. Regeneration is the work of the Holy Spirit, as a result of the effectual call, wherein He prepares the heart of the elect sinner to respond to the call of God. Citing the words of Christ to Nicodemus, Edwards told his hearers in a sermon on John 3:3, "Except a man be born again he cannot see the kingdom of God." This work of divine assistance is always efficacious. It is irresistible grace. The work of the Holy Spirit in the new birth is internal and supernatural. This is true in both the Old and New Testament eras, preached Edwards: "It is no wonder that Christ said that we must be born again."[19]

*Conversion:* As John Gerstner pointed out, sometimes Jonathan Edwards used the terms "effectual calling, conversion, repentance and regeneration [as] approximately synonymous terms."[20] But he also distinguished them. Edwards did teach that regeneration results in conversion, in which the elect sinner is brought into a filial and intimate relationship with God, through Christ: "There is such a thing as conversion." And this work of conversion is a great affect of God's power and grace in the

---

[18] Edwards, sermon on John 16:8.

[19] Edwards, sermon on John 3:7; see also Miscellany 617.

[20] Gerstner, *The Rational Biblical Theology of Jonathan Edwards*, III:149.

heart. Edwards believed and taught that conversion is
that work of God the Spirit whereby He graciously acts
upon the regenerated individual, causing him to respond
to the effectual call in faith and repentance.

Faith and repentance, although separate acts, are so
closely related that they cannot be temporally separated:
"So saving repentance and faith are implied in one another. They are both one conversion of the soul from sin
to God through Christ."[21] And in Miscellany 943, he put
it this way: "Repentance is often spoken of as the special
condition of remission of sins," and "remission of sins is
by faith in Jesus Christ," so "that faith and repentance
are not to be looked upon as properly two distinct
things"; rather, we should recognize "that evangelical
repentance is a certain exercise of faith in Jesus Christ."
Thus, "repentance is implied in faith."[22]

Repentance (*metanoia*), wrote Edwards, "signifies a
change of the mind." That is, the repentant sinner
changes his attitude toward sin and turns from it with a
holy hatred to serve God. There is a change or turning
from sin to God. The change of mind in repentance is
that in which saving faith is attained.

Edwards thus agreed with the Shorter Catechism's
definition of saving faith (Q. 86): "Faith in Jesus Christ is
a saving grace, whereby we receive and rest upon Him
alone for salvation, as He is offered to us in the gospel."
He wrote:

> The definition [of saving faith] might have
> been expressed in these words: faith is the
> soul's entirely adhering and acquiescing in the
> revelation of Jesus Christ as our Savior—Or
> thus: faith is the soul's embracing that truth of
> God that reveals Jesus Christ as our Savior—Or

[21] Edwards, *Works* (Yale), 8:331.
[22] Edwards, Miscellany 504.

> thus: faith is the soul's entirely acquiescing in, and depending upon, the truth of God, revealing Christ as our Savior.[23]

In his sermon on Matthew 13:5, on the Parable of the Sower, Edwards explained that there are various kinds of non-justifying faith spoken of in the Bible. Only one kind of faith is justifying faith. The kind of spurious faith which "rises only from superficial impressions is wont to whither away for want of root when it comes to be tried by the difficulties of religion."[24]

"Saving faith," on the other hand, "differs from all common faith in its nature, kind, and essence."[25] Genuine faith involves knowledge, assent, and trust. It is not enough to know the truth about Jesus Christ as presented in the gospel; nor is it sufficient to understand the message and merely assent to it in verbal agreement, as essential as these are. Saving faith "is the whole soul's active agreeing, according, and symphonizing with this truth." It is an "adhering to the truth, and acquiescing in it."[26] "Faith is a uniting with Christ, not a mere recognition of His existence."[27] "There is a difference," Edwards asserted, "between having a rational judgment that honey is sweet, and having a sense [taste] of its sweetness." The same is true with regard to saving faith: "There is a true sense of the divine and superlative excellency of the things of religion; a real sense of the excellency of God and Jesus Christ, and of the work of redemption, and the ways and works of God." There is "a true sense of the divine excellency of the things of God's

---

[23] Edwards, *Works*, II:580.
[24] See also Edwards, *Works*, II:585.
[25] Edwards, sermon on 1 John 1:5.
[26] Edwards, *Works*, II:580.
[27] Edwards, sermon on Galatians 5:6.

Word [which] does more directly and immediately convince us of their truth." When one has this sense, he ac-
quiesces to the "light of the glorious gospel of Christ."[28]

Moreover, at his conversion the elect child of God
has new desires and new habits infused into him by the
Spirit: "But man, when he is changed from a sinner to a
saint, has new principles of perception and action; principles that are entirely diverse and not arising merely
from [a] new disposition of the old or contracted habits as
those changes that are wrought by education do. They are
principles that are vastly superior to those he had before."[29] The new nature of man is "wrought in the heart
wholly by the Spirit," and it "dwells in the hearts of the
saints . . . as an inward, ardent, powerful principle of op-
eration."[30] This change affects the whole man. God becomes his best portion. He now "prefers God before all
other things, either in heaven or on earth."[31] In
Edwards's view, wrote Sang Lee, "God's Spirit comes to
dwell in the depth of the human mind and heart trans-
forming the imagination. Edwards asserts that the Spirit
of God must be 'infused' in the minds of the elect and
dwell in them as a new direction of their habit."[32]

---

[28] Edwards, sermon on Matthew 16:17.

[29] Edwards, sermon on John 3:3; see also his sermons on Ephesians
4:24 and Matthew 16:17.

[30] Edwards, sermon on Matthew 25:1–12.

[31] Edwards, sermon on Psalm 73:25. This sermon has been published in the Soli Deo Gloria title *The Puritan Pulpit: Jonathan
Edwards*.

[32] Lee, *The Philosophical Theology of Jonathan Edwards*, p. 143. When
Edwards used the word "infuse," he did so with regard to the process of sanctification. In justification, righteousness is imputed. But
in sanctification the Holy Spirit "infuses" grace. This is also the
teaching of the Westminster Larger Catechism (Q 77): "Although
sanctification be inseparably joined with justification, yet they differ, in that God in justification imputes the righteousness of Christ;

What this means, said Edwards in a sermon on Matthew 16:17, is that the Spirit "unites Himself with the mind of the saint . . . as a new supernatural principle of life and action." In fact, there is a sense in which we may even say, taught Edwards, that the Holy Spirit is the new principle Himself: "The Holy Spirit, or the third person of the Trinity, in His operations and fruits is the sum of the blessings that Christ purchased for us in the work of our redemption."[33] Herein consists true virtue.

In *The Nature of True Virtue*, Edwards argued that the essence of true virtue consists of a genuine love of being in general, which first and foremost must be rooted in a love for God. Or, as Samuel Logan explained, for Edwards, "true virtue involves a harmony between the will of the creature and the will of the Creator."[34] In Miscellany 567, Edwards wrote:

> If a man has any true love to God, he must have a spirit to love God above all, because, without seeing something of the divine glory, there can be no true love to God; but if a man sees anything of divine glory, he will see that He is more glorious than any other; for whereinsoever God is divine, therein He is above all others. If men are sensible only of some excellency in God that is common with Him to others, they are not sensible of anything of His divine glory. But so far as any man is sensible of excellency in God above others, so far must he love Him above all others.

---

in sanctification His Spirit infuses grace, and enables to the exercise thereof."
[33] Edwards, sermon on Galatians 3:13–14.
[34] Logan, "The Doctrine of Justification in the Theology of Jonathan Edwards," *Westminster Theological Journal* 46 (1984), pp. 48–49.

Further, a genuine love for God must be a love not primarily for what one receives from God, but for God Himself: "We are obliged not only to love Him with a love of gratitude for benefits received; but true love for God primarily consists in a supreme regard to Him for what He is in Himself."[35] Again, "The first objective ground of gracious affections, is the transcendently excellent and amiable nature of divine things, as they are in themselves, and not any conceived relation they bear to self, or self-interest."[36] This does not mean that there is not a proper type of self-love, because a biblically based self-love will see God as the highest good for the self, and will rejoice in and embrace God as the greatest good.[37]

*Justification:* Justification immediately follows conversion. To be justified is to be approved of God as a proper subject of pardon, with a right to eternal life. It is a legal act wherein God pardons the elect sinner and accepts him as righteous because the righteousness of Christ has been "imputed" to him.[38] In Miscellany 812, Edwards wrote:

---

[35] Edwards, *Works* (Yale), 3:144.

[36] Edwards, *Works*, I:317.

[37] Edwards, Miscellany 530. For more on this, see Piper, *Future Grace*, pp. 385–399.

[38] Theologians refer to this as the doctrine of "double imputation." That is, not only were the sins of the elect imputed to Christ (in His atoning cross work), but His righteousness was also imputed to them. In defense of the Edwardsean doctrine of justification, Robert Jenson wrote: "Edwards knows that the language of 'justification' is juridical language in Paul's use, and in the use of the Reformation, and he adheres to the rules of the metaphor. So also the justice given by God's justification is strictly an 'imputed' justice, in the purest style of . . . Calvinistic teaching: God chooses to reckon Christ's righteousness to the sinner, and so the sinner is judged righteous" (*America's Theologian*, p. 58).

> Justification is not only pardon of sin. . .but in
> an act or sentence approving of him as innocent
> and positively righteous, and so having a right to
> freedom from punishment, and to the reward of
> positive righteousness. . . . But the pardon we
> have in Christ is a freeing of persons from the
> punishment of sin as an act of justice, and be-
> cause they are looked upon and accepted as
> having that which is equivalent to innocence,
> viz., satisfaction. . . . Justification consists of
> imputing righteousness. To pardon sin is to
> cease to be angry for sin. But imputing righ-
> teousness and ceasing to be angry for sin are two
> things; one is the foundation of the other. God
> ceases to be angry with the sinner for his sin
> because righteousness is imputed to him.

The doctrine of justification by grace alone through
faith alone in Christ alone was the central doctrine of the
Reformation. Martin Luther considered it to be "the article by which the church stands or falls." John Calvin
declared it to be "the main hinge on which religion
turns" and "the sum of all piety." Edwards was a staunch
defender of this doctrine. Carl Bogue stated: "Jonathan
Edwards reflects the essence of the Scriptures when he
attributes salvation to the absolute sovereign grace of
God. The Reformation cry of *sola gratia* [by grace alone]
and *sola fide* [by faith alone] reverberates throughout his
writings."[39] Justification is by grace alone through faith
alone in Christ alone: "We are justified only by faith in
Christ, and not by any manner of goodness of our own."[40]

When Edwards taught that justification is by faith
alone, he did not mean that one's faith is in any sense
meritorious. Neither faith nor repentance justify "as a
work, for the nature of the one [repentance] is to re-

[39] Bogue, *Jonathan Edwards and the Covenant of Grace*, p. 209.
[40] Edwards, sermon on Romans 4:5.

nounce works, and the nature of the other [faith] is to depend on the work of another [Christ]."[41] "God does not give those that believe a union with or an interest in the Savior as a reward for faith," contended Edwards, "but only because faith is the soul's active uniting with Christ."[42] One's faith, he contended in Miscellany 1091, is not a work that merits him anything with God. In fact, "there is no good work," he wrote, "before conversion."[43] Faith means trusting in Christ alone, who justifies. The ground of justification is Christ's vicarious righteousness and sacrifice, i.e., His works.

Ultimately, of course, said Edwards, salvation is by works, but it is by Christ's works, not those of the believer: "If it is inquired what we must be saved for or on account of, the answer is it must be for works, but not our works; nor for any works that we have done or can do, but works that Christ has done for us."[44]

Jonathan Edwards did teach that faith and other graces (such as obedience and perseverance) are "conditions" of salvation. But they are non-meritorious conditions, because they all come as a gift of God. In a sermon on Romans 4:16 he preached: "In one sense of the word Christ alone performs the condition of our salvation. . . . And in another sense of the word there are other graces besides faith that are the condition of justification." But "faith is that in them which God has respect to upon the account of which God judges it meet that they should be looked upon as Christ's righteousness belonging to them. God sees it meet that some men rather than others should have Christ's righteousness imputed to them." Again:

---

[41] Edwards, Miscellany 620.
[42] Edwards, Miscellany 797.
[43] Edwards, Miscellany 797.
[44] Edwards, sermon on Genesis 6:22; see also his sermon on Romans 4:5.

"Faith itself is a gift of God, and that the saints' perseverance in a way of holiness unto glory is also the fruit of
electing love."[45] It is only by the power of the in-
dwelling Holy Spirit of God, he taught, that the saints are
enabled to persevere. And perseverance is so "contained
in the first act of faith," that it cannot possibly fail. By
God's grace, saving faith ushers in a certain "fitness" or
"suitableness," that (again, by God's grace) causes the
saint to persevere. As necessary as these graces are in order to salvation, they are gifts of God and are non-meritorious and non-justifying; they are not in any sense in-
strumental in justification. According to Edwards, "that
which makes our obedience the matter of our justification
. . . [is] contrary to the gospel doctrine of justification."[46]

Edwards's view here echoes that of the Westminster
Confession of Faith (16:2): "These good works, done in
obedience to God's commandments, are the fruits and
evidences of a true and lively faith."[47] The universal
obedience to which God calls us, said Edwards, "is the
proper evidence of our acceptable state" with God. As
taught in the Epistle of James, these works are a sign of
"manifestative justification" rather than "causal justification."[48] "Evangelical obedience . . . is an expression of
[saving] faith."[49]

On the other hand, Edwards denounced the Arminian
concept of conditions, wherein such conditions are to
some degree meritorious ("the Arminian scheme of justification by our own virtue"[50]). In Miscellany 2 he wrote:

---

[45] Edwards, sermon on 1 Peter 2:9.
[46] Edwards, Miscellany 474.
[47] In Miscellany 790, Edwards calls goods works the "proper evidences of godliness."
[48] Edwards, sermon on Romans 4:5.
[49] Edwards, Miscellany 670.
[50] Edwards, *Works* (Yale), 18:13.

"Talking thus, whether it be truly or falsely, is doubtless the foundation of Arminianism and neonomianism, and tends very much to make men value themselves for their own righteousness." And in a sermon on 1 Corinthians 1:29-31 he preached: "Whatever scheme is inconsistent with our entire dependence on God for all, and of having all of Him, through Him, and in Him, is repugnant to the design and tenor of the gospel and robs it of that which God accounts its luster and glory." Carl Bogue properly concluded that Edwards's "eye is clearly on the central Biblical truth that Christ fulfilled the condition of our righteousness and hence our justification." And, said C. C. Goen:

> Convinced that the doctrine of human ability which underlay the gradual shift to Arminian principles was a dangerous heresy, he preached a series of five sermons on justification by faith alone. These messages were broadsides of pure and uncompromising Reformed doctrine that all men justly deserve instant and total damnation, that none has a claim upon God's mercy, that salvation is a gracious gift of God through Jesus Christ who dies to save sinners, that it is appropriated through faith which itself is a gift of God—all these points were hammered home with a relentless force that scarcely can be appreciated by the reader today.[51]

*Adoption:* Like justification, adoption is a judicial act of God wherein He brings the justified sinner, as "partaking with Christ," into a filial relationship with Himself. All persons are not children of God, said Edwards. He would have nothing to do with the teaching of the broth-

---

[51] Cited in Bogue, *Jonathan Edwards and the Covenant of Grace*, p. 90, 88. The sermons to which Goen refers have been published by Soli Deo Gloria under the title *Justification by Faith Alone*.

erhood of all men and the universal fatherhood of God. It is only those who savingly receive Christ who are God's children.[52] They are the ones who have an intimacy of fellowship with the Father as His children.

*Sanctification:* John Gerstner wrote that "of the twelve hundred plus sermons which Edwards wrote, I estimate that sanctification was the central and most emphasized theme."[53] What Jonathan Edwards was expressing in his concept of these non-meritorious, non-justifying conditions of salvation is that even though salvation is by faith alone, that faith is not alone. If it is genuine faith, it is always accompanied by good works in the process of sanctification. Sanctification is a necessary corollary to justification.

According to Edwards:

> There is no room left for anyone to say that they have faith which justifies, and that they need take no care about works, and so to give themselves the liberty in sinning because they are not under the law but under grace; for though it is only faith that justifies, yet there is no faith that justifies but a working faith; so that it is impossible that any person should be saved without works as if they were justified upon the account of their works. It is as impossible that men should be saved without an evangelical, universal, and sincere obedience under the second covenant [of grace] as it was that they should be saved without a perfect obedience under the first covenant [of works].[54]

Said another way, "Men cannot be saved for any

---

[52] Edwards, sermon on John 1:12.
[53] Gerstner, *The Rational Biblical Theology of Jonathan Edwards*, III:224.
[54] Edwards, sermon on Galatians 5:6.

works of theirs, and yet they are not saved without works."[55] Again, "A true trust in Christ is never infused without other graces with it."[56] Further, the good works of the justified saint must be universal if a true conversion is involved, because a genuine conversion affects every area of the believer's life. And although all of his good works are tainted with sin, they are universal in scope: there is a "beautiful symmetry and proportion" of "holy affections," wherein the practice of godliness is the whole business of one's life. All is consciously done for the glory of God. "The spirit that godly men are of," preached Edwards, "is a spirit to be perfectly holy."[57] True godliness, then, "consists not in a heart to purpose to do the will of God, but in an heart to do it."[58]

The process of sanctification involves a constant warfare: there is a "mutual opposition and strife" that exists "between grace and corruption in the hearts of the saints during their continuance in this world."[59] The struggle in the life of the believer is likened to the struggle that went on in the womb of Rebecca between Jacob and Esau. This process includes the chastisement of

---

[55] Edwards, sermon on Genesis 6:22. John Calvin made a very similar statement in his commentary on Ezekiel 18:14–17: "But although works tend in no way to the cause of justification, yet when the elect sons of God were justified freely by faith, at the same time their works are esteemed righteous by the same gratuitous liberality. Thus, it still remains true that faith without works justifies, although this needs prudence and a sound interpretation; for this proposition, that faith without works justifies, is true and yet false according to the different senses which it bears. The proposition that faith without works justifies by itself is false, because faith without works is void."

[56] Edwards, sermon on Micah 3:11.

[57] Edwards, sermon on Psalm 119:3.

[58] Edwards, sermon on Deuteronomy 5:27–29.

[59] Edwards, sermon on Galatians 5:17.

God, who uses sickness and affliction to cause His saints to confess and forsake sin in their lives, that they may draw closer to Him.[60]

Here Edwards properly distinguished between one's initial conversion and later "conversions." There is only one conversion in the life of any Christian, which occurs when he responds in faith and repentance to the call of the gospel. At the same time, there must also be numerous "conversions" in a believer's life, which occur when he progressively confesses and forsakes sin in his life. In a sermon on Luke 22:32, Edwards taught that "those that have true grace in their hearts may yet stand in great need of being converted." Some of the signs of godliness, he taught, are those of "humility, a broken and contrite heart, a being poor in spirit, sensibleness of our own vileness and unworthiness, self-abasement, disclaiming all worthiness and glory, mourning for sin."[61]

This is why men must continue to "seek" after their conversion. Now, however, they are not seeking conversion, but for their continual growth in the Lord. In a sermon on Philippians 3:17, Edwards used the Apostle Paul as an example to Christians in this regard:

> The apostle did not only thus earnestly seek salvation before his conversion and hope, but afterwards as well. What he says in the third [chapter] of Philippians of his suffering the loss of all things, that he might be found in Christ,

---

[60] Edwards, sermons on Luke 4:38 and Ezekiel 7:16.

[61] Edwards, *Works* (Yale), 18:169n. Here (as elsewhere) we see Edwards's view of "the already and the not yet" aspect of soteriology. When a person is justified, he is already saved (2 Timothy 1:9). But there is a final aspect which is the "not yet" phase (Romans 13:11; 1 Peter 1:5). And in the meantime, man is in the process of "being saved" (1 Corinthians 1:18; Hebrews 10:14). Edwards did not use the phrase "already and not yet," but the idea is clearly there in his doctrine of sanctification. See Edwards, Miscellany 710.

and its being the one thing that he did to seek
salvation; and also what he says of his so running
as not uncertainly, but as resolving to win the
prize [1 Corinthians 9] of salvation, and keeping
under his body that he might not be a castaway
[1 Corinthians 9]; was long after his conversion
and after he had received his hope of his own
good estate.

If being already converted excuses a man from
seeking salvation any more, or makes it reasonable that he should leave off his earnest care and
labor for it, certainly the apostle might have
been excused when he had not only already attained true grace, but such eminent degrees of
it. To see one of the most eminent saints that
ever lived, if not the most eminent of all, so
exceedingly engaged in seeking his own salvation—it ought forever to put to shame those
that are a thousand degrees below him, and are
but mere infants to him, if they have any grace
at all; that yet excuse themselves from using
any violence after the kingdom of heaven now,
because they have attained already, easing themselves of the burden of going on earnestly to
seek salvation with this, that they have got
through the work, they have got a hope.

The apostle, as eminent as he was, did not say
within himself, "I am converted, and so am sure
of salvation. Christ has promised it to me; what
need I care any further about obtaining salvation? Yea, I am not only converted, but I have
obtained great degrees of grace." The apostle
knew that though he was converted, yet there
remained a great work that he must do, in order
to his [final] salvation. There was a narrow way
to eternal glory, that he must pass through and
never could come to the crown of glory any
other way. He knew that it was absolutely necessary for him earnestly to seek salvation still;
he knew that there was no going to heaven in a
lazy way.

According to Jenson, Jonathan Edwards would have us know that the whole life of sanctification can be synopsized by two principles. The first is a holiness of heart, which will "keep men from errors in judgment about religion." The reason being "that the sanctified mind is let into the spiritual world," where it "perceives what ideas are harmonious" with the things of God and which are not. The second is the realization that "the motives to believers to perform the commands of God are not because salvation is [upon] the condition of doing them . . ., but the amiableness of God . . . the loveliness of virtue, and its natural tendency to happiness."62

Holiness, taught Edwards, is both the desire and the goal of the saint. He delights in holiness out of a love for God, who is the ultimate producer of holiness: "Holiness is . . . the highest beauty and amiableness. . . . It makes the soul a little sweet and delightful image of the blessed Jehovah. . . . What a sweet calmness, what calm ecstasies, does it bring to the soul. . . . It makes the soul like . . . a garden planted by God . . . where the sun is Jesus Christ, the blessed beams and calm breeze, the Holy Spirit."63

As seen earlier, Edwards taught that the process of sanctification necessarily involves the usage of the means of grace: (primarily) Scripture, the sacraments, and prayer. It is not possible for a Christian to grow spiritually without a knowledge of the Word of God. Therefore, he said in a sermon on Hebrews 5:12, "every Christian should make a business of endeavoring to grow in knowledge of divinity. . . . There is no other way by which any means of grace whatsoever can be of any benefit, but by knowledge. . . . Christians ought not to

---

62 Jenson, *America's Theologian*, p. 87. Jenson here quotes from Miscellanies 141 and 79.
63 Edwards, Miscellany a. This was Edwards's first entry in the Miscellanies.

content themselves with such degrees of knowledge in divinity as they have already obtained. It should not satisfy them that they know as much as is absolutely necessary to salvation, but should seek to make progress. . . . However diligently we apply ourselves, there is room enough to increase our knowledge of divinity, without coming to an end." Christians, then, must grow in knowledge. "If persons have ever tasted the sweetness of the Word and grace of Christ they will be longing for more and more of it."[64] And all knowledge is conveyed by the Spirit of God to the elect of God by means of the Word and the sacraments (as they are explained and understood in accordance with the Word).[65] "God's Spirit," said Edwards, "always attends His ordinances."[66]

Then too, said Edwards, prayer is essential to the process of sanctification. In His Word, God speaks to His people; in prayer, they speak to Him. Herein there is communion between God and His elect. Prayer, of course, is the duty of all men, but only the regenerate can truly pray.[67] For God's people, there is "the great duty of secret prayer." "The true spirit of prayer is no other than God's own Spirit dwelling in the hearts of the saints. That being a Spirit that comes from God, does naturally tend to God in holy breathings [and] pantings. . . . True prayer is nothing else but faith expressed. . . . True prayer is the faith and reliance of the soul breathed forth

---

[64] Edwards, sermon on 1 Peter 2:2.

[65] Edwards, sermon on Hebrews 5:12. Edwards taught that the means of grace, by themselves, have no influence to produce grace. Rather, they supply the mind of man "with matter for grace to act upon when God [the Holy Spirit] shall be pleased to infuse it." It is the Spirit of God alone who "causes acts of grace in the soul; and that grace [comes] as immediately from Him" (Miscellany 539).

[66] Edwards, *Works*, I:539.

[67] Edwards, sermon on Nehemiah 1:3–4.

in words."[68] Genuine prayer is God's children talking to their heavenly Father.

Finally, Edwards taught, even though there will be no more sin to wage war against in the final state, the process of sanctification will continue forever:

> There are many reasons to think that what God has in view, in an increasing communication of Himself through eternity, is an increasing knowledge of God, love to Him, and joy in Him. And it is to be considered that the more those divine communications increase in the creature, the more it becomes one with God; for so much the more it is united to God in love, the heart is drawn nearer and nearer to God, and union with Him becomes more firm and close, and at the same time the creature becomes more and more conformed to God. The image is more and more perfect, and so the good that is in the creature comes for ever nearer and nearer to an identity to that which is in God. In the view therefore of God, who has a comprehensive prospect of the increasing union and conformity through eternity, it must be an infinitely strict and perfect nearness, conformity, and oneness. For it will for ever come nearer and nearer to that strictness and perfection of union which there is between the Father and the Son.[69]

*Perseverance:* The doctrine of the perseverance of the saints is not one and the same thing with assurance of salvation. Whereas perseverance teaches that no Christian will finally fall away from the state of salvation to which God has brought him, assurance has to do with the individual Christian's confidence of his own state. A justified man may doubt his salvation, but this does not deny the

---

[68] Edwards, sermon on Job 27:10.
[69] Edwards, *Works*, I:101.

doctrine of perseverance.

Jonathan Edwards contended that perseverance is a condition of salvation. Perseverance in holiness is absolutely necessary to salvation because a genuine saving faith is a persevering faith. "It is necessary," he said, "for those that have religious affections and seem to have a love to Christ that they should endure to the end in order to their being saved."[70] Perseverance "is the only way to heaven, the narrow way that leads to life."[71]

And yet it is not possible that a genuine Christian will not persevere. The reason being that "God, in the act of justification, which is passed on a sinner's first believing, has respect to perseverance as being virtually contained in that first act of faith."[72] God's promise of acceptance is made only to a persevering sort of faith. The believer is in union with Jesus Christ, and he cannot ever permanently fall away from the faith. A true Christian may indeed fall into sin, but God will keep him from continuing in it. "That the saints shall surely persevere will necessarily follow this," that "the righteousness by which they have justification unto life" has "already been performed for them [by Christ] and imputed to them" in Christ.[73]

*Assurance:* As stated by John Gerstner: "It may be clear enough that, according to Edwards, if you have it [salvation] you cannot lose it, but the great question still remains, How do you know if you have it?"[74] Edwards believed that there were certain marks of a work of the Spirit that reveal a genuine work of conversion. Herein "true grace [is] distinguished from the experience of

---

[70] Edwards, sermon on Matthew 24:12–13.
[71] Edwards, sermon on Isaiah 35:8.
[72] Edwards, *Works*, II:596.
[73] Edwards, *Works*, II:597.
[74] Gerstner, *Jonathan Edwards, Evangelist*, p. 166.

devils."[75] "Assurance is not to be obtained," he taught, "as much by self-examination as it is by action."[76] Edwards preached a series of ten sermons (as yet unpublished) on "The Parable of the Virgins" on this very subject. In this series he showed from the Word of God both "wherein true and false Christians agree," and "wherein true and false Christians differ." And the difference is literally a difference between heaven and hell.

*Religious Affections* is undoubtedly Edwards's fullest treatment of this subject. It is "probably the most penetrating analysis of Christian inward experience ever written."[77] Regarding this work, in his book *God's Passion for His Glory* (p.59), John Piper wrote of it:

> This book is the mature, seasoned reflection of Edwards, and the most profound analysis of the difference between true and false Christian experience that emerged from the season of the Great Awakening. In fact, it is probably one of the most penetrating and heart-searching Biblical treatments ever written of the way God works in saving and sanctifying the human heart.

A reading of *Religious Affections*, along with his other teachings on the subject of assurance,[78] reveals that Edwards was in agreement with the Westminster Larger Catechism (Q. 80–81):

> Such as truly believe in Christ, and endeavor to walk in all good conscience before Him, may,

[75] Edwards, sermon on James 2:19.
[76] Edwards, sermon on 1 Corinthians 9:26.
[77] Hulse, *Who Are the Puritans? And What Do They Teach?*, p. 143.
[78] See, for example, Edwards, *Works* (Yale), 16:227–228, 327–338. See also the collection of Edwards sermons published under the title *The True Believer*, by Soli Deo Gloria.

without extraordinary revelation, by faith
grounded upon the truth of God's promises, and
by the Spirit enabling them to discern in
themselves those graces to which the promises
of life are made, and bearing witness with their
spirits that they are the children of God, be infallibly assured that they are in the estate of
grace, and shall persevere therein unto salvation. . . . Assurance of grace and salvation, not
being of the essence of faith, true believers
may wait long before they obtain it; and after
the enjoyment thereof, may have it weakened
and intermitted, through manifold distempers,
sins, temptations, and desertions; yet are they
never left without such a presence and support
of the Spirit of God as keeps them from sinking
into utter despair.

*Glorification:* In a sermon on Revelation 5:5–6 ("The
Excellency of Christ"), Edwards preached that "Christ
has brought it to pass that those whom the Father has
given Him should be brought into the household of God;
that He and His Father, and His people, should be as one
society, one family, that the church should be as it were
admitted into the society of the blessed Trinity."

Glorification is the final phase of the *ordo salutis*,
which, according to Edwards, comes in two stages. The
first stage begins at the death of the individual Christian,
when he enters into the disembodied, intermediate state;
the second stage occurs at the time of the final resurrection of the dead.[79]

Stage one begins with the death of the saint, when he
is ushered into the presence of God, in Christ:

Death is not only no death for them, but is a
translation to a more glorious life, and is turned
into a kind of resurrection from the dead. Death

---

[79] Edwards, *Works*, II:888–905.

> is a happy change to them, and a change that is
> by far more like a resurrection than a death. It
> is a change from a state of much sin, and sor-
> row, and darkness, to a state of perfect light,
> and holiness, and joy. When a saint dies, he
> awakes, as it were, out of sleep. This life is a
> dull, lifeless state; there is but a little spiritual
> life, and a great deal of deadness; there is but a
> little light, and a great deal of darkness; there is
> but a little sense, and a great deal of stupidity
> and senselessness. But when a godly man dies,
> all this deadness, and darkness, and stupidity,
> and senselessness are gone forever, and he en-
> ters immediately into a state of perfect life, and
> perfect light, and activity, and joyfulness.[80]

"There is nothing upon earth," preached Edwards, "that will suffice to represent to us the glory of heaven."[81] In heaven the elect of God will realize the "peculiar comfort" of the communion of the saints. They will recognize one another, and enjoy this fellowship throughout eternity. But the *summum bonum* of glorification is that "the saints in heaven will see God. They shall not only see that glorious city [the heavenly Jerusalem], and the saints there, and the holy angels, and the glorified Christ; but they shall see God Himself . . . with the eye of the soul."[82]

In a sermon on Psalm 27:4, Edwards preached that a good man "loves God above all else for His own beauty." In heaven, the good man sees God face to face. This is the "beatific vision," which surpasses all other blessings that the saints will have in their final, heavenly state. Here on this earth, there are times when God gives His people views of His beauty and excellency. And these are more

---

[80] Edwards, *Works*, II:891.
[81] Edwards, sermon on Revelation 21:18.
[82] Edwards, *Works*, II:900.

precious to them than all the treasures of the wicked. But in the heavenly kingdom the saints will see God. This beatific vision consists mainly in a view of the glorified Jesus Christ, the second person of the Godhead:

> [T]hat beatific vision that the saints will have of God in heaven is in beholding the manifestations that He makes of Himself in the work of redemption. For that arguing of the being and perfection of God that may be *apriori* does not seem to be called seeing God in Scripture, but only that which is by manifestations God makes of Himself in His Son. All other ways of knowing God are by seeing Him in Christ the Redeemer, the image of the invisible God, and in His works; or, the effects of His perfections in His redemption and the fruits of it (which effects are the principal manifestation or shining forth of His perfections). And in conversing with them by Christ which conversation is chiefly about those things done and manifested in this work, if we may judge by the subject of God's conversation with His church by His Word in this world. And so we may infer that business and employment of the saints, so far as it consists in contemplation, praise, and conversation is mainly in contemplating the wonders of this work, in praising God for the displays of His glory and love therein, and in conversing about things appertaining to it.[83]

Moreover, preached Edwards in a sermon on Revelation 18:20, the saints in heaven will not grieve over the lost[84]; rather, it will be just the opposite: "When the saints in glory see the wrath of God executed on ungodly men, it will be no occasion of grief to them, but

[83] Edwards, Miscellany 777.
[84] Edwards, *Works* (Yale), 11:70.

of rejoicing."[85] Even Christian parents will delight in
the punishment of their incorrigible children, the reason
being, that the saints will rejoice that God's justice is
being carried out, and His majesty revealed. They will
rejoice over the fact that God is righting all wrongs and
making His power known. The saints will love God as
He is worthy to be loved, and honor Him as He is
deserving to be honored; and they will do so with
sinless hearts and sinless love. In the words of John
Piper: "It is not that suffering is pleasant to God and the
saints itself, but that the vindication of God's infinite
holiness is cherished so deeply."[86]

The second stage of glorification begins at the time of
the final resurrection:

> As the wicked have not their full punishment
> until after the resurrection, so neither have the
> saints their complete happiness. Though they
> have attained to such exceeding glory, yet they
> are not yet arrived at its highest degrees, for
> that is reserved for their final state. The reward
> which the saints receive after the resurrection
> is often spoken of as their chief reward. . . . So
> the happiness that they shall be given at
> Christ's second coming is spoken of as the
> principal happiness.[87]

It is natural for us to want to be embodied, taught
Edwards. The non-corporeal state, in this sense, is un-
natural: "Redemption is not complete till the resurrection. . . . So long as the separation between soul and body

---

[85] The sermon is titled "The End of the Wicked Contemplated by
the Righteous" or "The Torments of the Wicked in Hell No
Occasion of Grief to the Saints." It is included in the collection
entitled *The Wrath of Almighty God*, published by Soli Deo Gloria.
[86] Piper, *The Pleasures of God*, p. 75.
[87] Edwards, *Works*, II:893–894.

remains, one of those evils remains that is a part of the
penalty of the law. . . . To be without a body is in itself
an evil, because it is a want of that which the soul of man
naturally inclines to and desires."[88]

The bodies of Christians will be raised both "in an
exceeding strength" and "in a wonderful beauty, for we
are told that their bodies shall be like to Christ's glorious
body."[89] These same resurrected and glorified saints
"shall sit on thrones with Christ, to judge wicked men
and angels." And "Christ shall pronounce the blessed
sentence upon them: 'Come, ye blessed of My Father,
inherit the kingdom prepared for you from the foundation
of the world.' "[90] In this glorified state, the saints will
see that "the eternal heaven surrounds Christ not merely
as an house surrounds an inhabitant . . . but rather as
plants and flowers are before the sun, that have their life
and beauty and being from the luminary."[91]

There are degrees of blessedness in heaven, preached
Edwards in a sermon on John 14:2. There are many
mansions in God's heavenly kingdom. All of the saints
are like vessels that are filled to the brim with joy; yet,
the vessels are of different sizes. "The happiness of the
saints shall never have any interruption," and the degree
of the blessedness of the saints "will be according to the

---

[88] Edwards, Miscellany 644.

[89] In Miscellanies 806 and 809, Edwards taught that the bodies of
Christians in the final state will be the same bodies which they had
prior to their death, only now glorified. Thus he agrees with the
Westminster Confession of Faith (32:2), that "at the last day, such
as are found alive shall not die, but be changed: and all the dead shall
be raised up, with the self-same bodies and none other, although
with different qualities, which shall be united again to their souls
forever."

[90] Edwards, *Works*, II:895–896.

[91] Edwards, Miscellany 1122.

degree of their holiness and good works."[92]

Then, too, there will be continual growth in purity, with no sin or corruption to interfere in any way. It is certain that the inhabitants of heaven do increase in their knowledge. And "there shall never be any end to their glory and blessedness. Therefore it is so often called eternal life, and everlasting life. . . . The pleasures which there are at God's right hand are said to be for evermore (Psalm 16:11)." "As God is eternal, so their happiness is eternal; as long as the Fountain lasts, they need not fear but they shall be supplied."[93] God's "saints will be progressive in knowledge and happiness to all eternity."[94]

At this time, when the body of Christ's church is perfect and complete, then "will be the marriage supper of the Lamb." This day will be glorious, not only for the church, but for Christ as well: "It will be the day of the gladness of Christ's heart; [and] the feast, and pomp, and holy mirth, and joy in this marriage day will be continued to all eternity." The bride will then be presented by "Christ to God the Father . . . and God shall be all in all; and the glory of God [the Father] and the glory of His Son shall be displayed in heaven in a more abundant manner than ever before."[95] This, concluded Edwards, is the end for which God created the world, i.e., that He be glorified. And "if God's chief end is the manifestation of His glory," wrote John Gerstner, "where is that fully realized so well as in heaven?"[96]

Finally, it is noteworthy that, in the thought of Jonathan Edwards, just as there are two spiritual worlds, the elect and the reprobate, so there are two material

---

[92] Edwards, Miscellany 617.
[93] Edwards, *Works*, II:902.
[94] Edwards, Miscellany 435.
[95] Edwards, *Works*, II:896.
[96] Gerstner, *Jonathan Edwards on Heaven and Hell*, p. 41.

worlds, which are everlasting. This present world, which is the lower world, will be the locus of hell; and "the whole world shall [be] a furnace of the fiercest and most raging heat."[97]

The new heavens and new earth, however, will be brand new:

> The remedy that is promised in Christ is a new heaven and a new earth, a new and much better habitation and state of things. . . . This restoration is equivalent to a resurrection of heaven and earth, and is more than a mere restoration: for it shall be a far more glorious state of things, not only than is immediately before the dissolution or conflagration [of the old world], but more glorious than the state of the world was before the Fall, as the resurrection of the bodies of the saints is more than a mere restitution . . . . Hence, this new state of things is called a new heaven and a new earth. Christ came to restore all things with respect to the elect that, whatever there is of the ruinous effects of the Fall through the whole universe, all might be fully and perfectly healed in Christ; that old things might pass away and all things become new; that man himself might be a new creature, both in his soul in conversion and sanctification, and in his body by the resurrection, and the world as to him might become a new creation; and so not only himself created anew in Christ Jesus, but everything created anew as to Him fully and perfectly. Revelation 21:5: "Behold, I make all things new."[98]

---

[97] Edwards, *Works* (Yale), 9:509.
[98] Edwards, Miscellany 806.

# Bibliography

Augustine, Aurelius. *The Retractions.* Translated by Sister Mary Inez Bogan. Washington, DC: Catholic University of America Press, 1968.

Berkhof, Louis. *Systematic Theology.* Grand Rapids, Mich.: William B. Eerdmans Publishing Company, 1941, 1979.

Bogue, Carl W. *Jonathan Edwards and the Covenant of Grace.* Cherry Hill, N.J.: Mack Publishing Company, 1975.

Brand, David C. *Profile of the Last Puritan: Jonathan Edwards, Self-Love, and the Dawn of the Beatific.* Atlanta, Ga.: Scholars Press, 1991.

Budgen, Victor. *The Charismatics and the Word of God.* Darlington, England: Evangelical Press, 1989.

Calvin, John. *Come Out from among Them.* Edited by Kevin Reed. Translated by Seth Skolnitsky. Dallas, Tex.: Protestant Heritage Press, 2001.

Calvin, John. *Commentaries.* Vols. I–XXII. Grand Rapids, Mich.: Baker Book House, 1981.

Calvin, John. *Institutes of the Christian Religion.* Vols. I and II. Library of the Christian Classics. Edited by John T. McNeill. Translated by Ford Lewis Battles. Philadelphia, Pa.: Westminster Press, 1960.

Calvin, John. *Sermons on Deuteronomy.* Edinburgh: Banner of Truth Trust, 1987.

Cherry, Conrad. *Jonathan Edwards: A Reappraisal.* Gloucester, Mass.: Peter Smith, 1974.

Clark, Gordon H. *Karl Barth's Theological Method.* Unicoi, Tenn.: The Trinity Foundation, 1997.

Clark, Gordon H. *Religion, Reason, and Revelation.* Unicoi, Tenn.: The Trinity Foundation, 1995.

Clark, Gordon H. *The Atonement.* Unicoi, Tenn.: The Trinity Foundation, 1987.

Crampton, W. Gary. "A Biblical Theodicy," in *Christ the Mediator.* Dallas, Tex.: Blue Banner Ministries, 2000.

Crampton, W. Gary and Richard E. Bacon, *Built Upon the Rock.* Dallas, Texas: Blue Banner Ministries, 1999.

Crampton, W. Gary and Richard E. Bacon. *So Great a Salvation.* Dallas, Tex.: Blue Banner Ministries, 2001.

Crampton, W. Gary and Richard E. Bacon. *Toward a Christian Worldview.* Dallas, Tex.: Blue Banner Ministries, 2000.

Crampton, W. Gary. *The Scripturalism of Gordon H. Clark.* Unicoi, Tenn.: The Trinity Foundation, 1999.

Dodds, Elisabeth. *Marriage to a Difficult Man.* Philadelphia, Pa.: Westminster Press, 1971.

Edwards, Jonathan. *A Jonathan Edwards Reader.* Edited by John E. Smith, Harry S. Stout, and Kenneth P. Minkema. New Haven, Conn.: Yale University Press, 1995.

Edwards, Jonathan. *Charity and Its Fruits.* Edinburgh: Banner of Truth Trust, 1852, 1986.

Edwards, Jonathan. *Images or Shadows of Divine Things.* Edited by Perry Miller. New Haven, Conn.: Yale University Press, 1948.

Edwards, Jonathan. *Jonathan Edwards on Knowing Christ.* Edinburgh: Banner of Truth Trust, 1990.

Edwards, Jonathan. *Jonathan Edwards: Representative Selections.* Edited by C. H. Faust and T. H. Johnson. New York: Hill and Wang, 1962.

Edwards, Jonathan. *The Experience That Counts.* Prepared by N. R. Needham. London: Grace Publications Trust, 1991.

Edwards, Jonathan. *The Works of Jonathan Edwards.* John E. Smith and Harry S. Stout, general editors. New Haven, Conn.: Yale University Press. (hereafter, *Works* [Yale]):

> Volume 1: *Freedom of the Will.* Edited by Paul Ramsey. 1957.
> Volume 2: *Religious Affections.* Edited by John E. Smith. 1959.
> Volume 3: *Original Sin.* Edited by Clyde A. Holbrook. 1970.
> Volume 4: *The Great Awakening.* Edited by C.C. Goen. 1972.
> Volume 5: *Apocalyptic Writings.* Edited by Stephen J. Stein. 1977.
> Volume 6: *Scientific and Philosophical Writings.* Edited by Wallace E. Anderson. 1980.

Volume 7: *The Life of David Brainerd.* Edited by
    Norman Pettit. 1985.
Volume 8: *Ethical Writings.* Edited by Paul Ramsey.
    1989.
Volume 9: *A History of the Work of Redemption.* Edited
    by John F. Wilson. 1989.
Volume 10: *Sermons and Discourses, 1720-1723.* Edited
    by Wilson H. Kimnach. 1992.
Volume 11: *Typological Writings.* Edited by Wallace E.
    Anderson, Mason I. Lowance, Jr., and
    David H. Watters. 1993.
Volume 12: *Ecclesiastical Writings.* Edited by David D.
    Hall. 1994.
Volume 13: *The Miscellanies a-500.* Edited by Thomas
    A. Schafer. 1994.
Volume 14: *Sermons and Discourses, 1723-1729.* Edited
    by Kenneth P. Minkema. 1997.
Volume 15: *Notes on Scripture.* Edited by Stephen J.
    Stein. 1998.
Volume 16: *Letters and Personal Writings.* Edited by
    George S. Claghorn. 1998.
Volume 17: *Sermons and Discourses:* 1730-1733. Edited
    by Mark Valeri. 1999.
Volume 18: *Miscellanies 501-832.* Edited by Ava
    Chamberlain. 2000.

Edwards, Jonathan. *Selections from the Unpublished Writings
of Jonathan Edwards.* Alexander Grosart, ed. Ligonier,
Pa.: Soli Deo Gloria Publications, 1992.

Edwards, Jonathan. *Standing in Grace.* Morgan, Pa.: Soli
Deo Gloria Publications, 2002.

Edwards, Jonathan. *The Wrath of Almighty God.*
Morgan, Pa.: Soli Deo Gloria Publications, 1996.

Edwards, Jonathan. *The Puritan Pulpit: Jonathan Edwards.* Morgan, Pa.: Soli Deo Gloria Publications, 2004.

Edwards, Jonathan. *The Works of Jonathan Edwards* (hereafter, *Works*), 2 vols. Edited by Edward Hickman. Edinburgh: Banner of Truth Trust, 1834, 1984.

Edwards, Jonathan. *The Works of President Edwards* (hereafter *Works* [Worcester]), 8 vols. Edited by Samuel Austin. Worcester, Mass.: Isaiah Thomas, 1808-1809.

Erickson, Millard J. *Christian Theology.* Grand Rapids, Mich.: Baker Book House, 1983-1985.

Fiering, Norman. *Jonathan Edwards's Moral Thought in Its British Context.* Chapel Hill, N.C.: University of North Carolina Press, 1981.

Fiering, Norman. *Moral Philosophy at Seventeenth Century Harvard.* Chapel Hill, N.C.: University of North Carolina Press, 1981.

Gerstner, Edna. *Jonathan and Sarah: an Uncommon Union.* Morgan, Pa.: Soli Deo Gloria Publications, 1995

Gerstner, John H. *Jonathan Edwards on Heaven and Hell.* Morgan, Pa.: Soli Deo Gloria Publications, 1998.

Gerstner, John H. *Jonathan Edwards: A Mini-Theology.* Morgan, Pa.: Soli Deo Gloria Publications, 1996.

Gerstner, John H. *Jonathan Edwards, Evangelist.* Morgan, Pa.: Soli Deo Gloria Publications, 1995.

Gerstner, John H. *The Rational Biblical Theology of Jonathan Edwards.* Powhatan, Va.: Berea Publications;

Orlando, Fla: Ligonier Ministries, 1991–1993.

Gerstner, John H. *The Theology of Jonathan Edwards: A Study Guide.* Grand Rapids, Mich.: Outreach Inc., 1987.

Hefley, James C. *Studies in Genesis.* Scripture Press Adult Series. Edited by Roy Irving. Wheaton, Ill.: Scripture Press Publications, 1981.

Hodge, Charles. *Systematic Theology*, vols. I–III. Grand Rapids, Mich.: Eerdmans Publishing Company, 1977.

Hulse, Erroll. *Who Are the Puritans? And What Do They Teach?* Darlington, England: Evangelical Press, 2000.

Jenson, Robert W. *America's Theologian.* New York: Oxford University Press, 1988.

Lee, Sang Hyun. *The Philosophical Theology of Jonathan Edwards.* Princeton, N.J.: Princeton University Press, 1988.

Logan, Samuel T., Jr. "The Doctrine of Justification in the Theology of Jonathan Edwards." *Westminster Theological Journal* 46 (1984). Philadelphia, Pa.: Westminster Theological Seminary, 1984.

Manspeaker, Nancy. *Jonathan Edwards: A Bibliographical Synopsis.* Lewiston, N.Y.: E. Mellen Press, 1981.

McDermott, Gerald R. *Jonathan Edwards Confronts the Gods.* New York: Oxford University Press, 2000.

McDermott, Gerald R. *One Holy and Happy Society.* University Park, Pa.: Pennsylvania State University Press, 1992.

Miller, Perry. *Jonathan Edwards*. New York: Meridian, 1959.

Morgan, Irvonwy. *The Godly Preachers of the Elizabethan Church*. London: Epworth Press, 1965.

Murray, Iain H. *Jonathan Edwards: A New Biography*. Edinburgh: Banner of Truth Trust, 1987.

Nichols, Stephen. J. *Jonathan Edwards: A Guided Tour of His Life*. Phillipsburg, N.J.: Presbyterian and Reformed Publishing, 2001.

Packer, J. I. *A Quest for Godliness*. Wheaton, Ill.: Crossway Books, 1990.

Packer, J.I. *English Puritan Theology*. An audio cassette series. Orlando, Fla.: Ligonier Ministries, 1988.

Piper, John. *Future Grace*. Sisters, Ore.: Multnomah Press, 1995.

Piper, John. *God's Passion for His Glory*. Wheaton, Ill.: Crossway Books, 1998.

Piper, John. *The Pleasures of God*. Portland, Ore.: Multnomah Press, 1991.

Piper, John. *The Supremacy of God in Preaching*. Grand Rapids, Mich.: Baker Book House, 1990.

Reese, W. L., ed. *Dictionary of Philosophy and Religion*. Atlantic Highlands, N.J.: Humanities Press, 1980.

Reymond, Robert L. *A New Systematic Theology of the Christian Faith*. Nashville, Tenn.: Thomas Nelson

Publishers, 1998.

Reymond, Robert L. *Introductory Studies in Contemporary Theology*. Philadelphia, Pa.: Presbyterian and Reformed Publishing Company, 1968.

Reymond, Robert L. *Paul: Missionary Theologian*. Ross-shire, Great Britain: Christian Focus Publications, 2000.

Reymond, Robert L. *The Reformation's Conflict with Rome: Why It Must Continue*. Ross-shire, Great Britain: Christian Focus Publications, 2001.

Rolston, Holmes, III. *John Calvin Versus the Westminster Confession*. Richmond, Va.: John Knox Press, 1972.

Schaff, Philip. *The History of the Christian Church*. Grand Rapids, Mich.: W. B. Eerdmans Publishing Company, 1988 (reprint).

Scheick, William. *The Writings of Jonathan Edwards: Theme, Motif, and Style*. College Station, Tex.: Texas A & M University Press, 1975.

Singer, C. Gregg. *John Calvin: His Roots and Fruits*. Greenville, S.C.:, A Press, 1989.

Smith, Chard Powers. *Yankees and God*. New York: Hermitage House, 1954.

Sproul, R. C., John H. Gerstner, and Arthur Lindsley. *Classical Apologetics*. Grand Rapids, Mich.: Zondervan Publishing House, 1984.

Steele, David N. and Curtis C. Thomas. *The Five Points of Calvinism*. Phillipsburg, N.J.: Presbyterian and Reformed

Publishing Company, 1963.

Stoddard, Solomon. *A Guide to Christ*, Morgan, Pa.: Soli Deo Gloria Publications, 1993.

Strong, Augustus H. *Systematic Theology*. Valley Forge, Pa.: Judson Press, 1907, 1985.

Townsend, Harvey G. *The Philosophy of Jonathan Edwards*. Eugene, Ore.: The University Press, 1955.

Warfield, Benjamin B. *Studies in Theology*. Edinburgh: Banner of Truth Trust, 1988.

# Books in Print by Jonathan Edwards

**Soli Deo Gloria Publications**

*Altogether Lovely: The Beauty and Glory of Jesus Christ*

*Pressing into the Kingdom*

*The Wrath of Almighty God*

*To All the Saints of God*

*The True Believer*

*Our Great and Glorious God*

*The Puritan Pulpit: Jonathan Edwards* (2004, containing 16 sermons unpublished in Edwardss' lifetime)

*Devotions from the Pen of Jonathan Edwards*

*Standing in Grace: A Treatise on Grace*

*The Freedom of the Will*

*Justification by Faith Alone*

**The Banner of Truth Trust**

*The Works of Jonathan Edwards* (2 vol. Hickman Edition. No edition of Edwards's works is complete. Even this standard set contains only about 10–15% of what Edwards wrote!)

*A History of the Work of Redemption*

*Charity and Its Fruits*

*The Religious Affections*

*Jonathan Edwards on Knowing Christ*

*Jonathan Edwards on Revival*

**Yale University Press**

Volume 1: *Freedom of the Will*
Volume 2: *Religious Affections*
Volume 3: *Original Sin*
Volume 4: *The Great Awakening*
Volume 5: *Apocalyptic Writings*
Volume 6: *Scientific and Philosophical Writings*
Volume 7: *The Life of David Brainerd*
Volume 8: *Ethical Writings*
Volume 9: *A History of the Work of Redemption*
Volume 10: *Sermons and Discourses, 1720-1723*
Volume 11: *Typological Writings*
Volume 12: *Ecclesiastical Writings*
Volume 13: *The Miscellanies a-500*
Volume 14: *Sermons and Discourses, 1723-1729*
Volume 15: *Notes on Scripture*
Volume 16: *Letters and Personal Writings*
Volume 17: *Sermons and Discourses: 1730-1733*
Volume 18: *Miscellanies 501-832.*
Volume 19: *Sermons and Discourses, 1734–1738*
Volume 20: *The Miscellanies, 833–1152*
Volume 21: *Writings on the Trinity, Grace, and Faith*
Volume 22: *Sermons and Discourses, 1739–1742*

**International Outreach**

*Seeking God*

*Knowing the Heart*

**Broadman and Holman**

*The Blessing of God*